SOBER INTOXICATION OF THE SPIRIT

PART TWO

Sober Intoxication of the Spirit
Part Two
Born Again of Water and the Spirit

Raniero Cantalamessa, O.F.M., CAP.

TRANSLATED BY MARSHA DAIGLE-WILLIAMSON

PUBLISHED BY ST. ANTHONY MESSENGER PRESS
CINCINNATI, OHIO

Cover design by Candle Light Studios
Cover image © Cover image by Iakov Kalinin | Shutterstock
Book design by Mark Sullivan

LIBRARY OF CONGRESS CATALOGING-IN-PUBLICATION DATA
Cantalamessa, Raniero.
[Sobria ebbrezza dello Spirito. English]
Sober intoxication of the Spirit : born again of water and the spirit / by
Raniero Cantalamessa ; translated by Marsha Daigle-Williamson.
p. cm.
ISBN 1-61636-321-5(pbk. : alk. paper)
1. Pentecostalism—Catholic Church—Meditations.   I. Title.
BX2350.57C3613 2005
234'.1—dc22
2005015042

Published by Servant Books
an imprint of St. Anthony Messenger Press.
28 W. Liberty St.
Cincinnati, OH 45202
www.AmericanCatholic.org
www.ServantBooks.org

Printed in the United States of America.
Printed on acid-free paper.
12 13 14 15 16   5 4 3 2 1

CONTENTS

PREFACE

This second volume of *Sober Intoxication of the Spirit* is, like the first volume, a collection of teachings given at conferences of the Catholic charismatic renewal conferences. However, any reader, looking at the titles of the individual chapters, will see that the topics treated here would be of interest not only to people in the charismatic renewal but to all believers in Christ.

Cardinal Leo Suenens, one of the four moderators of the Second Vatican Council, used to say that the charismatic renewal is a "stream of grace" destined to "pour itself out" into the "larger body"—that is, into the whole Church—and that afterward it could then disappear. These chapters, in fact, do not deal with any kind of new spirituality or with any particular "charism" like those that distinguish a religious order or an ecclesial movement. They deal with Christian life as St. Paul conceived of it: life "in Christ" or—what signifies the same thing for him—life "in the Spirit."

The Holy Spirit, I always like to say, does not make new things, but he makes all things new: He does not speak new words and does not institute new sacraments, but he makes the words of Jesus come alive and makes the sacraments he instituted efficacious.

An Orthodox bishop (not someone in the charismatic renewal) once said the following, which everyone in the Church should meditate on:

> Without the Holy Spirit:
> God is far away,
> Christ stays in the past,
> the Gospel is a dead letter,
> the Church is simply an organisation,
> authority a matter of domination,
> mission a matter of propaganda,
> liturgy no more than an evocation,
> Christian living a slave morality.
> But with the Holy Spirit:
> the cosmos is resurrected and groans with the birth-pangs
> of the Kingdom,
> the risen Christ is there,
> the Gospel is the power of life,
> the Church shows forth the life of the Trinity,
> authority is a liberating service,
> mission is a Pentecost,
> the liturgy is both memorial and anticipation,
> human action is deified.[1]

I am grateful to Servant Books for the opportunity to share these reflections with my brothers and sisters in the United States and in other English-speaking countries. So often have they and I joined in deep prayer and joyful proclamation of the gospel. I am glad to share these reflections with them especially because I am indebted to them: It was in the United States—New Jersey, to be precise—that, in 1977, I myself received the grace of "the baptism of the Spirit."

CHAPTER ONE

Conversion

I will develop this topic in two parts. In the first part I will attempt to illustrate the meaning of the word "conversion" (*metanoia*) in Jesus' preaching in the gospel. In the second part I will attempt to explain the meaning of conversion in apostolic teaching. I mean not that the apostles preached a conversion different from the one Jesus preached but that they found themselves preaching to a group of people who were different from those whom Jesus addressed throughout his life. Jesus was preaching to people who still needed to make a radical decision to enter the kingdom, and he preached to them so that they would make that decision. The apostles spoke of conversion but to people who had already entered the kingdom, people who had already converted to the gospel and had lived many years as part of the Church. In the apostles' preaching, the need for a *second conversion* emerged that we must look at very carefully because, in many ways, it applies to those of us who have lived our whole lives in the Church and for some period of time in the charismatic renewal. However, this second conversion cannot be understood, let alone occur, without people having initially understood and experienced the first conversion spoken of in the gospel.

Conversion in the Gospel

Let us begin by looking at conversion in the gospel. Conversion, understood in its strict sense as the joyful proclamation brought by Jesus that the kingdom of God has come among men, begins with these words: "The time is fulfilled, and the kingdom of God is at hand; repent, and believe in the gospel" (Mark 1:15).

The theme of conversion is not new; it is spoken about throughout the Old Testament and especially by the prophets. The need for conversion was preached even in the Judaism of Jesus' time, and John the Baptist, the last of those prophets, was preparing the way for Christ by preaching conversion: "Repent, for the kingdom of heaven is at hand" (Matthew 3:2), and "I baptize you with water for repentance" (Matthew 3:11a).

A comparison with conversion in the Old Testament and Judaism, including that of John the Baptist, shows the absolute novelty of the conversion preached by Jesus. The novelty consists in the strict connection between converting and believing in the gospel. This new conversion leads to faith and, moreover, consists in faith—that is, in accepting the gospel.

Prior to Jesus' teaching, "to convert" usually meant to change one's life, to change one's conduct, to "prepare the way of the Lord, / make his paths straight" (Matthew 3:3), so that the Lord could come to an individual. In other words, to convert meant to merit salvation, to hasten salvation; it had an ascetic and moral meaning. This conversion primarily involved the faithful observance of the law through one's own strength. The law held the highest place, at least in the minds of the people (scribes, Pharisees) with whom Jesus dealt.

With Jesus, that dynamic is now turned upside down. Conversion and salvation have changed places: Conversion is no longer first, followed by salvation, but, on the contrary, salvation comes first, and then conversion. "To convert" now means to believe the good news ("gospel") that salvation is offered to people as the free gift of God; it means seizing the kingdom that has come and leaving everything else behind in exchange for it. Therefore, in Jesus' preaching, "to convert" means "to make a decision," and it is a "decisive choice" because everything depends on it.

The meaning and the content of this radical decision gets clarified throughout the gospel. In Matthew 13, we find two short parables in which that decision is compared two figures—to a man who sells all he has so he can acquire the treasure hidden in a field and to a merchant who renounces his whole collection of precious stones to buy the pearl of great price (see Matthew 13:44–46). That same idea is presented, in the negative, in the episode of the rich young man: He lacked the courage to leave everything in exchange for the kingdom, which is identified here as a person, Jesus. The rich young man missed the greatest opportunity of his life! (see Mark 10:17–22; Matthew 19:16–22; Luke 18:18–25).

In the gospel, the requirements of conversion are radical: One must be prepared to renounce everything, including health and physical life: "If your right eye causes you to sin, pluck it out" (Matthew 5:29a). Everything—privileges, accomplishments, and merits gained in the kingdom—and even God's gifts! It is significant that, toward the end of his preaching, Jesus returned to speaking explicitly about conversion to the disciples who had followed him. In that context, "to convert" is the equivalent of "to become like children":

> At that time the disciples came to Jesus, saying, "Who is the greatest in the kingdom of heaven?" And calling to him a child, he put him in the midst of them, and said, "Truly, I say to you, unless you turn [change] and become like children, you will never enter the kingdom of heaven." (Matthew 18:1–3)

Detachment from spiritual gifts and privileges—spiritual directors know what these words mean! People must be prepared to start over again at the beginning, without any reliance on or security in anything except the pure love of the Father. They must become like children who, when they ask for something, do not have a consciousness of "deserving" it because of their efforts but a consciousness that is naturally instilled in them that their fathers and mothers love them. That is their basis for security, and they are right to assume it.

Gifts can become a kind of security and lead to pride and a feeling of superiority, as was the case with the apostles when they were discussing among themselves who the greatest was. Perhaps this is

the most urgent kind of conversion for some of us: to stop lever-
aging our past experiences, our charisms, and our service to a group
or to the whole charismatic renewal and to start over at the beginning, with God alone as our treasure—like "newborn infants" (1 Peter
2:2) or the man who is overtaken by the kingdom while he is in the
field and does not turn back to get his cloak (see Matthew 24:18).
So many difficulties due to secret rivalries and human comparisons
would disappear from our groups, and the work of God would shine
forth more brilliantly if only our pride were destroyed.

This is conversion in the gospel: leaving everything behind for
the sake of the kingdom—that is, Jesus himself—leaving everything
behind to possess the One who is Everything!

An example of the perfect gospel conversion occurs with the apostle
Paul. In his conversion there is an external, dramatic aspect that we all
know about: Saul falls to the ground and hears a voice saying, "Saul,
Saul, why do you persecute me?" (Acts 9:4b). But there is also an
internal aspect, more hidden and quiet, which unfolds little by little
afterward. In Philippians 3, from verse 3 on, the apostle describes this
interior process of conversion as being like a path that led him at a
certain point in his life to consider all that he ever was and all that
he had ever done as "loss," as "refuse," in comparison to possessing
the one unique thing, Christ Jesus: "Indeed I count everything as loss
because of the surpassing worth of knowing Christ Jesus my Lord"
(Philippians 3:8a).

Here Paul models for us—for us, in the renewal—that subsequent
conversion that entails detachment from one's past service to Jesus in

the Church. This detachment is necessary for us to avoid becoming entangled again in our own righteousness and to be able, instead, to flow freely with the grace and with the Spirit who always wants to make things new. In fact, Paul repeats, "Brethren, I do not consider that I have made it [perfection] my own; but one thing I do, forgetting what lies behind and straining forward to what lies ahead, I press on toward the goal for the prize of the upward call of God in Christ Jesus" (Philippians 3:13–14).

Applying the conversion that the gospel speaks about to us, we can say that it consists in handing oneself over totally and definitively to the grace of God, in surrendering the reins of one's life. (This was the image that accompanied my decision to receive the "baptism of the Spirit.") It consists in saying with one's whole heart, "I want God and nothing else!" In practical terms, it is a surrender of one's liberty to God, a matter of saying, "I will say yes to whatever you want!" This is the most stubborn obstacle, as we will soon see, for the old man cries out with all his strength, "Everything, but not my freedom!" St. Augustine knew this struggle between the two wills, between the old man and the new man, and he had to pull himself away from his old man in order to thrust himself into the arms of God who was inviting him: "Cast yourself on him. He will not draw back and let you fall."[2]

Perhaps there are some among us who find ourselves in the same situation as Augustine. On one hand, you are attracted by the desire for a new life and for the joy you see in the brothers and sisters; on the other hand, you are still held back by old habits and the fear that if you convert you would have to renounce this or that thing. To help you, even this helps only one of you, I want to read the passage in which the great convert from Hippo describes his final struggle between the flesh and the spirit:

> I upbraided myself much more bitterly than ever before. I twisted and turned in my chain [a sinful relationship] until it might be completely broken...but still held by it I was. Within the hidden depths of my soul, O Lord, you urged me on. By an austere mercy you redoubled the scourges of fear and shame, lest I give in again, and lest that thin little remaining strand...should grow strong again and bind me yet more firmly.
>
> Within myself I said: "Behold, let it be done now, now let it be done," and by those words I was already moving on to a decision. By then I had almost made it, and yet I did not make it.... The nearer came that moment in time when I was to become something different, the greater terror did it strike into me. Yet it did not strike me back, nor did it turn me away, but it held me in suspense.
>
> My lovers of old, trifles of trifles and vanities of vanities, held me back. They plucked at my fleshly garment, and they whispered softly: "Do you cast us off?" and "From that moment we shall no more be with you forever and ever!"... But now by far less than half did I hear them.[3]

In that internal struggle, this thought was of great help to Augustine: He considered the group that had followed Christ—young people, children, soldiers, the elderly—and he said to himself, "If these men and these women, why not me?" I want to say the same thing to any person I was speaking about before. Look around you; look at the thousands of brothers and sisters with radiant faces and resolutely say to yourself, "If these men and these women, why not me?" "How long will I keep saying 'tomorrow, tomorrow?' Why not now? Why can't this hour be the hour to mark the end of my sad and useless life apart from God?"[4] Perhaps in the past you have sprinted to try to jump over the moat, your own Red Sea, in order to find yourself in the freedom of the Promised Land and out of Egypt. But your nerve weakened and you stopped at the brink and remained on this side, on the border of Egypt. The Lord invites you to have confidence not in yourself but in his Holy Spirit. With him, you can do it. Take the leap and do not stop until you are in the arms of the Father, who is waiting for you.

Conversion in Apostolic Teaching

Now let us make an imaginary leap from Jesus' time to the time of the early Church. Let us go from the shores of the Sea of Galilee, where Jesus earlier spoke to crowds, and come to Asia Minor, where, at the end of the first century, were Christian churches consisting of people who had received the Good News some time ago. These people had converted a first time and were now living the new life in Christ. I chose the region of Asia Minor because I will be using the seven letters to the churches in Asia (see Revelation 2–3) as the point of departure for my reflections.

The problem or fundamental concern that lay behind these letters is clear and can be articulated this way: how to awaken the initial

fervor—or, as it says in the text, "the first love"—in Christian communities that had lost it and ran the risk of becoming lukewarm. Let us
hear how the problem of conversion is handled in this specific milieu,
because it is clear that it applies to people who are many years down
the road from their beginning, or conversion, and feel that they, too,
are in danger of becoming lukewarm, of slackening. The admonition
"He who has an ear, let him hear what the Spirit says to the churches,"
which appears at the end of each of the seven letters (Revelation 2:7a,
11a, 17a, 29; 3:6, 13, 22), is now addressed to us: "Let anyone who has
an ear listen to what the Spirit is saying to us today!"

The seven letters in Revelation have a very similar structure. Let us
listen to two of them first before I begin my commentary: the letter
to the Church at Ephesus (Revelation 2:1–7) and the letter to the
Church at Laodicea (Revelation 3:14–22).

In all seven letters Jesus is speaking and is given new titles: "the
First and the Last," "Son of God," the "Amen." He exhorts everyone,
saying, "I know your works!" He follows this with his approval for
good works done in the community and then his disapproval for their
evil deeds. At this point, in five of the seven letters, he issues a solemn
call to conversion: "*metanoēson*," "be converted!" or, as some of the
translations prefer to say, "repent!"[5]

But there is something new here. In the Gospels, Jesus said, "Repent
and believe," but here the same Jesus, now resurrected, says, "Repent
and do good works"! In fact, there are many similar sayings in those
letters: "Remember then from what you have fallen, repent and do
the works you did at first" (Revelation 2:5a); "I have not found your

9

works perfect…. repent" (Revelation 3:2–3); "Be zealous and repent" (Revelation 3:19b).

The first conversion, spoken about in the Gospels, was a conversion *from works to faith*. The conversion that apostolic teaching speaks about to us now seems to be, in contrast, a conversion *from faith to works*. This is mystifying. Are we perhaps returning to the Old Testament? Are we abandoning the pure faith of the gospel for good works? Absolutely not! The apostle Paul, as we all know, is the chief defender of salvation by faith and not by works (see Galatians 2:16–19; Romans 3:28); he himself explains to us what this Christian "conversion to works" means.

He calls the former works, done under the law, "works of the flesh," while he calls the works to be done by believers now, done under the rule of grace, "fruits of the Spirit" (see Ephesians 5:8–13; Galatians 5:18–23). There is a big difference between the conversion to good works preached by the Church and the one preached in the Old Testament. The good works now are no longer commanded as the condition and cause of salvation but as *consequences* of salvation. We no longer say, "Do this and that *so that* you will be saved," but "Do this and that *because* you are saved." Good works are the logical consequence, the natural expression, of the salvation received from Christ. They do not imply a falling away from a new life and a return to the old life of slavery.

These good works are not the fruits of the flesh—that is, products of purely human effort—but of the Spirit who stirs up both desire and action in us and who asks us only for docility, free consent, and cooperation. St. Paul combines in the same text a condemnation of good works—as the cause of salvation—and an exhortation to good works—as a consequence and fruit of the salvation effected by Jesus: "For by grace you have been saved through faith; and this is not your own doing, it is the gift of God—not because of works, lest any man should boast. For we are his workmanship, created in Christ Jesus for good works, which God prepared beforehand, that we should walk in them" (Ephesians 2:8–10).

This apostolic teaching about the fruits of conversion, or the fruits of the Spirit, is based on the teaching of Jesus himself, who called them "good fruits." He once said, "Every tree that does not bear good fruit is cut down and thrown into the fire" (Matthew 7:19). The fig tree that had leaves but no fruit and that Jesus cursed was a symbol for the person who stops at the first conversion without adding the second conversion of bearing fruit (see Mark 11:12ff). Jesus' discourse on the vine and the branches contains this same thought. Once grafted into the vine and receiving life from the vine, the branches should bear fruit or they will be pruned: "Every branch of mine that bears no fruit, he [the Father] takes away, and every branch that does bear fruit he prunes, that it may bear more fruit" (John 15:2).

Second Conversion

We need to recall these foundational teachings because there is uncertainty and confusion here and there. There are people who, having discovered the great Pauline truth that we are freely saved not by works but by faith in Christ, have stopped at this point without taking the last step, which is absolutely indispensable, toward the fruits of conversion. The insidiousness of being lukewarm hides here. It obscures certain traditional values that have always nourished the true holiness of the Church—values like the mortification of the flesh, the denial of self, vigilance over one's senses and instincts, and the ascetic effort for purification from sin. Such people have understood that they are not made holy *by* these things (and they are right about that), but they have not understood that they cannot become holy *without* these things. The Catholic understanding of faith requires that both these aspects be present together. That is why I said that the second conversion is a conversion from faith to works—that is, from faith alone to faith "working through love" (Galatians 5:6), faith that expresses itself in works.

The danger that is highlighted here has an ancient name, because it represents a recurring temptation in the story of Christian spirituality. It is called "quietism," the belief that God's grace operates in us by itself and that we need only abandon ourselves to it passively, remaining quiet and inactive like a boat that lets itself drift on the waves of the sea.

Another danger similar to this is that of illuminism, which bases action on an interior illumination by the Spirit, or an illumination believed to be such, while disregarding other criteria (tradition and hierarchy) for truth normally observed by the Church.

In his letters to the churches in Asia, John highlights among the unrighteous works that can lead a community astray the people who go after private, strange doctrines that no one else holds and who see these as the central nucleus of the faith. They are the followers of the doctrine of Balaam and of the Nicolaitans (evidently, private doctrines of pseudo-enlightened people that ended with their fabricators because every trace of them was soon lost). The pastoral epistles vigorously denounce this plague of false teachers who teach private doctrines and find ready followers among simple-minded and foolish people who cannot distinguish good doctrine from bad (see 2 Timothy 2:16–18; 3:6–9).

The danger of illuminism and of false doctrines finds a correlation today in the excessive attention given to private revelations here and there and to strange, new devotions. They take the focus away from the real issue of conversion and often harm the cause of the Church by turning people to fantastic and dubious phenomena, causing them to depart from what is essential in faith and to concentrate instead on secondary things.

In addition to the danger of false teachers, John highlights the danger of false prophets. In the letter to the church at Thyatira, Jesus says, "But I have this against you, that you tolerate the woman Jezebel, who calls herself a prophetess and is teaching and beguiling my servants" (Revelation 2:20). It is not—note well—Jezebel who is being reproved but the community who lets her operate, perhaps through fear of her manipulations or her apocalyptic threats or simply through their desire for a quiet life. This warning should also be taken seriously by groups: These things impede an authentic spiritual revival and lead a community to fall under God's judgment (see Revelation 2:22ff).

These are some of the bad fruits that John highlights in the churches and that I have wanted to highlight because it seems to me they are still present and very challenging to discern. But I do not want us to stop at this negative point. We are interested primarily in knowing the good fruits of the Spirit so that we can cultivate them and become zealous for them.

What, concretely, are these good fruits of the Spirit? In practice, all of the new life in Christ is a fruit of the Spirit. But St. Paul lists some fruits in particular: "love, joy, peace, patience, kindness, goodness, faithfulness, gentleness, self-control" (Galatians 5:22–23). The fruit that encompasses all the others is the one listed first: love, *agapē*. Love is the "new commandment" that makes human beings new singers of the new canticle and men and women of the new covenant. It is the fruit par excellence of the Spirit, so much so that, wherever love is, it encompasses everything: "Make love your aim" (1 Corinthians 14:1a).

We need, in short, to carry out the transition from what is described in 1 Corinthians 12 to what is described in chapter 13—that is, the transition from the charisms to the fruits of the Spirit. Moving from charisms to fruits of the Spirit does not mean abandoning charisms to focus on fruits but joining charisms to fruits, undergirding the charisms with the fruits of the Spirit! We need to move from the sporadic exercise of this or that charism—or even of all of the charisms (supposing someone had all of them)—to a charismatic life, one permanently lived in the Spirit, minute by minute. Holiness has a connection with this second approach but not with the first. A fruit of the Spirit is a *gratia gratum faciens*, which makes one pleasing to

God; a charism is a *gratia gratis data* that, in an extreme case, can even lead me to hell. The Gospel, in fact, speaks of people who have done miracles in Jesus' name but to whom he is forced to say, in the end, "I never knew you; depart from me" (Matthew 7:23).

The strength and spiritual influence of some people is very different from that of others. Some, who base themselves only on the use of charisms, can accomplish things in the power of the Spirit that will diminish, however, if their spiritual life does not support the exercise of those charisms. Others, having become or trying to become "conformed to the image of his Son" (Romans 8:29), acquire a stabilizing power as they are transformed in Christ. In all that they do and say, the power of the Spirit shines forth, and others convert merely by seeing them pray. This is the conversion, or the further step, that is necessary, especially for those who have been involved in the charismatic renewal for some time.

As long as we are merely content to receive and use the gifts of the Spirit, the charisms, we will be like Christmas trees, with glittering gifts set out there at night by Dad and Mom. But every Christmas tree, after a while, withers and is thrown out, because it is not a living tree; it has finished serving after it has given the children joy.

When we begin to practice the life in the Spirit (love, ongoing repentance, and mortification), then we will look like a real tree, rooted in the earth and bearing fruit in due time:

> He is like a tree
> planted by streams of water,
> that yields its fruit in its season,

and its leaf does not wither.

In all that he does, he prospers. (Psalm 1:3)

The "streams of water" alongside which this tree grows represent the water that Jesus has given us: the Holy Spirit (see John 7:37–39). This real, living tree must undergo, like actual fruit trees, defoliation in winter, pruning in spring, and heat in summer—that is, it must go through the cross. One fruit tree in particular furnishes us with a particularly eloquent image: The cacao tree is a tree that bears fruit only in its last season, in late autumn. In order to bear its golden fruit, however, it must lose all its leaves. Finally, now barren in the field, we can see its beautiful fruits from a distance. But the tree that produced them no longer exists, so to speak; it no longer has its beauty or dignity. It reminds us of the special tree that carried the fruit of salvation for all: the tree of the cross! Let anyone who has an ear hear.

Do we want to be Christmas trees, perhaps not even real ones but plastic ones, or do we want to be living trees? We know the difference.

The gospel has spoken of conversion as a decision, and apostolic teaching has spoken of conversion as an awakening. But there is still one important thing to be said: The result of conversion is joy! Conversion is beautiful; it is the greatest joy a man can experience. The man who found a treasure hidden in his field went "in his joy" (Matthew 13:44) to sell everything he had; on the other hand, the rich young man who lacked the courage to make the leap "went away sorrowful" (Matthew 19:22). To convert is to be with the Bridegroom, so how can we be sad or how can we fast while the Bridegroom is present?

But there is something even more extraordinary in conversion than a person's own joy: the joy of God! "There will be…joy in heaven over one sinner who repents" (Luke 15:7). This is a mystery: I can make my God happy or diminish his happiness. God is not completely happy while there is still anyone outside the door who refuses to enter, be it the prodigal son or the elder brother.

How can one resist this thought? How can we not immediately say, "Today, this very day, I want to convert"?

Jesus, draw us to follow after you to the Father!

CHAPTER TWO

"Then You Will Know That I Am"

A nd the haughtiness of man shall be humbled, / and the pride of men shall be brought low; / and the LORD alone will be exalted in that day" (Isaiah 2:17). In this verse from the word of God, "that day" means "this very day." Today, the haughtiness of man must be brought low and the Lord alone must be exalted!

When we gather together at Easter Vigil, we look like a great procession of lights or an enormous torchlight procession that enters a church: Everyone has his own candle. There are so many little lights that are moving. The little light that each of us holds is our "I." Everyone has a role that sets him or her apart and makes him or her visible: someone presides, someone sings, someone prays, someone preaches. The angels, who discern spiritual reality on all occasions, witness a sea of fluttering lights.

But then the omnipotent word of God summons us all to extinguish the lights so that there might be one single Light among us. The Easter candle in the darkened church is lit as a symbol of Christ risen from the dead, and then the Lord, and only he, is truly exalted. Then, just as it happened when the temple of Solomon was dedicated (see 1 Kings 8:11b), the glory of God will come down and fill that place.

For some time now, there has been a word that I sense I must proclaim to the Church; it has been entrusted to me, and in a certain sense I am responsible for it. It was a gift due to the prayers of some cloistered sisters. There are several cloistered monasteries who have received the grace of the charismatic renewal as a whole community, adapting it to their particular vocation, and now they are the most beautiful flowers hidden at the heart of the charismatic renewal itself. They received from the renewal, but they give even more in return to the renewal with their silent prayer and their docility to the Spirit. Some time ago, shortly before Easter, I was celebrating Mass in one of these monasteries. The text for the Gospel Reading, John 8, included the verse in which Jesus says, "When you have lifted up the Son of man, then you will know that I am he [Greek: "I am"], and that I do nothing on my own authority but speak thus as the Father taught me" (John 8:28).

The fact that the words "I am" were written with capital letters in my lectionary was the spark that provoked an unexpected revelation. These two words, in fact, "exploded" inside me. Since that day I feel them resonating inside and outside of me, in time and beyond time, like a majestic and solemn melody: It is the cry of the Risen One who proclaims, "I AM, I AM!" That experience led to a personal Easter for me. Now I must make you hear that cry; I am not sure how to succeed in doing that with my very limited abilities, but I must do it. I cry out to all of you in the name of Jesus, "*Ephphatha!* Open yourselves up! Open yourselves up to receive this cry from Jesus that saves you." It establishes the truth of all things, because the real truth about all things is that God "is" and that man "is not"; God is everything, and man, without God, is nothing.

I am convinced that this cry of the Risen One, "I AM," has something important to say to us at this very point in our history. But first let us try to understand its meaning better in the light of the Gospel of John and the rest of the Bible.

Jesus often uses the expression "I AM" in the Gospel of John, and it almost always refers to the event of the cross: "When you have lifted up the Son of man"—that is, when you will have crucified him—"then you will know that I AM!" All of the Gospel of John can be described as a long preparation for the scene at Calvary. Everything is oriented to that "hour," beginning with the exclamation of John the Baptist, "Behold the Lamb of God" (John 1:29). In chapter 13 of this same Gospel, we read, "I tell you this now, before it takes place [he is speaking of his betrayal and his death], that when it does take place, you may believe that I am he" (John 13:19). In John 18:4–5, the Gospel writer reports this dialogue at the time of Jesus' arrest:

"Whom do you seek?" They answered him, "Jesus of Nazareth." Jesus said to them, "I am he!" [Here and elsewhere

the English translation says, "I am he," but in the original
Greek it is always the same expression, *Egō eimi,* which
means simply, "I am."]...When he said to them, "I am he" ["I
AM!"], they drew back and fell to the ground. (John 18:4–6)

It was those two words, "I AM," that made his enemies draw back and
fall to the ground because of the dazzling power of the Divine Being,
who, at least for an instant, was free to manifest himself.

But what is so unique and mysterious about these two words? Why
are they written with capital letters in some Gospel translations? It is
really only a subject, "I," and a verb, "am." This is the simplest propo-
sition in any human language, as basic as bread in relation to other
food. The secret is that "I AM" is the name of God, and, according to
the Bible, the mystery of his Person and his power is enclosed in that
name. We never say these two words alone; we say, "I am a man, I am
a woman, I am tired, etc." We never just say, "I am." Only God can say
that without adding anything.

"I AM WHO I AM!" God said to Moses, and added, "Thus you shall
say to the sons of Israel, 'I AM has sent me to you'" (Exodus 3:14–15,
NAB). The meaning of this divine name is "I am he who truly exists,
he who is, who is alive, who saves." This is the opposite of idols who
have no substance outside the mind of man.

But listen to how God explains his name in certain passages in the
Bible. In the Song of Moses, in Deuteronomy, we read:

Where are their gods...?

...

Corinthians 1:30); "Peace to all of you that are in Christ" is Peter's closing line (1 Peter 5:14). To live in Christ, not in ourselves, means partaking in the very Being of Jesus himself.

This should instill in us a desire to not live for ourselves, to detach our egotistical "I" from the things we say and do, to the point of considering "I" almost a "third person." We need to lose interest in that "I" and become interested in our true "I," which is Christ. We need to put to death "the worm" that spoils all our fruits.

A Word for the Charismatic Renewal

I said at the beginning that Jesus' "I AM" has something to say to us today, and we need to understand what it is. It is not difficult; we simply need to understand what the temptation of eating from "the tree of the knowledge of good and evil" (see Genesis 2:9ff) is for us at this point. It is a sign of health and vitality that when we find ourselves in times of crises we let ourselves be judged by the word of God. We need to have the courage to let ourselves be admonished by the Lord: "But when we are judged by the Lord," writes Paul, "we are chastened so that we may not be condemned along with the world" (1 Corinthians 11:32). It is not the case that some are vindicated by this judgment and some are condemned, because only the word of God comes forth victoriously. We are all judged and reproved, myself first of all. Let us humble ourselves, therefore, under the mighty hand of God, so that he may be exalted, and he will exalt us in due time!

The temptation of eating from the tree of the knowledge of good and evil is a matter of wanting to be something in and of ourselves, focusing on ourselves, relying on ourselves, and, little by little, diverting our gaze from the sun to look at the shadow. When we focus on ourselves—talk about ourselves, defend ourselves—we are focusing on the shadow and not on the sun, who is Christ the Lord. At this very time, we can be either people who focus on the sun or people who focus on the shadow.

St. Paul wrote, "God chose what is low and despised in the world, even things that are not, to bring to nothing things that are" (1 Corinthians 1:28). We must choose whether we want to be people who are humanly "nothing," who could be used by God "to bring to nothing things that are," or whether, instead, we want to become people who "are"—who are esteemed, who make ourselves felt, who are strong in numbers and in organization and sociologically relevant—who enjoy advantages that will be inexorably brought to nothing by God.

Unfortunately, there is something inevitable in all of this. Once the work of God—every work of God—has entered into history and has been put in the hands of men and women, it tends to become more and more a work of human beings; prophecy tends to become institutionalized. That is what happened to the church of the Galatians.

But this did not prevent the apostle—and it should not prevent us—from crying out with an equally great grief, "Why so quickly? Are you so tired of walking on the water of pure faith that you are all now doing works again? Your own works!" In the words of Paul, "O foolish Galatians!... Are you so foolish? Having begun with the Spirit, are you now ending with the flesh? Did you experience so many things in vain?" (Galatians 3:1, 3–4).

I frankly do not know what "ending with the flesh" means concretely, so we need to discover that together. I know, however, that this danger hangs over all of us. Therefore, like a sentinel, I sound the alarm so that the fateful day would at least be delayed, so that God would remain among us as the only Lord, the only Sovereign, as long as possible, and so that the Lord and "only he!" would be exalted.

I have asked myself sometimes what in some of the prayer groups and budding communities that are rising up here and there in the charismatic renewal pleases Jesus so much that he would manifest so much power and so many wonders in them. It seemed to me that the secret of what makes them so precious to God is their absolute poverty, the fact that they have no past and hardly any future. They are almost a "nothing," like certain life forms that appear in the morning and disappear in the evening, reabsorbed into the great bosom of life, or like a little cloud that calmly disappears from the sky after having poured out all its water.

Traditional religious orders have a past, often a glorious one; recent ones (lay institutes, ecclesial movements) have a future and are sometimes very aware of it. God is looking for something very, very small among so many grand and established groups (which do please him and are useful to him), something that he can take just as it is, without having to be concerned about its past or its future. He is looking for something that will be useful to him, for an instant, something unencumbered that wants nothing and asks for nothing in return for pleasing God and for making his power and his wishes shine forth in the world.

Do we want to be that small thing that is precious to God? Do we want to be that instrument of "nothing" in his omnipotent hand? Then, let us not worry about "setting up house"; let us not worry about assuring that the charismatic renewal has a future among today's ecclesial realities; let us not worry about numbers.

Let it be enough for us that the future of the Church is already assured. Let the Church be enough for us, as *institution*. For our part, let us try, if we can, to remain prophetic for the Church, even if it is only in small measure. Let us continue to draw directly from the Church, especially from the local Church, all that is necessary to live a life of the Spirit—sacraments, authority, ministries, and doctrine. Let us continue to pour out all that we are, even though we are small, directly into the bosom of life that is the Church—quietly or also openly, if it is possible and if it is requested. Let us try to be that little cloud, ready to disappear, after it has poured out all its water on the Church.

I see what happens to the institutes and religious orders that have a past to carry forward. Much of their energy (sometimes all of it) is committed to maintenance and upkeep (houses and works to oversee, recruits needing formation) without much left over to pour back into the common treasury of the Church. We are not asked "to economize" but to spend all for the Church right away.

I had hardly come into contact with the charismatic renewal when, one day in prayer, I was struck with certain thoughts. I seemed to sense the new thing the Lord was doing in the Church through the charismatic renewal. I took a sheet of paper and a pen and wrote down some thoughts, which surprised me, as they came without premeditation:

The Father wants to glorify the Son, Jesus Christ, on earth in a new way, through a new intervention. The Holy Spirit is appointed to carry out this glorification because it is written, "He will glorify me and take that which is mine." A Christian life entirely consecrated to God, without a founder, without a rule, and without new congregations. The Founder: Jesus! The Rule: the gospel interpreted by the Holy Spirit! The Congregation: the Church! Do not worry about tomorrow, do not try to make something that will remain, and do not set in motion recognized organizations that can be perpetuated by successors.... Jesus is a Founder who never dies, so there is no need for successors. We always need to let him do new things, even tomorrow. The Holy Spirit will remain in the Church, even tomorrow!

Not to "End with the Flesh"

I said earlier that I did not know exactly what "to end in the flesh" means. All the same, we can point out certain dangers to guard against that could, because of their consequences, make us fall back into old ways. The main danger is that of "domesticating" the charismatic renewal and the Spirit himself. The renewal brought everyone— some more, some less—into the experience of the holiness of God as "a devouring fire" (see Isaiah 30:30). In fact, we can even say that the charismatic renewal in the Catholic Church was born from an experience of that kind. One of the participants on the famous Duquesne weekend (1967) described afterward the experience of the group gathered together in the chapel:

> Fear of the Lord welled up within us; a fearful awe kept us from looking up. He was personally present and we feared being loved too much. We worshiped him, knowing for the first time the meaning of worship. We knew a burning experience of the terrible reality and presence of the Lord that has since caused us to understand at first hand the images of Yahweh on Mt. Sinai as it rumbles and explodes with the fire of his Being, and the experience of Isaiah 6:1–5, and the statement that our God is a consuming fire. This holy fear was somehow the same as love or evoked love as we really beheld him. He was altogether lovely and beautiful, yet we saw no visual image. It was as though the splendorous, brilliant, personal God had come into the room and filled both it and us.[6]

But a human being cannot long remain in this atmosphere and this presence that judges all and lays all bare. He is moved to exclaim, in the words of Isaiah, "Who among us can dwell with the devouring fire? / Who among us can dwell with everlasting burnings?" (Isaiah 33:14b). Unable to withstand this devouring fire, what should a sinful man do? He domesticates it—that is, he puts a fence around it and keeps it at a distance. He returns to things that are easier to handle. The fire is put "under a bushel," and the bushel consists of a multitude of human words and initiatives. Man retakes the upper hand, little by little, with his futile bustling around. Then the ideological phase blossoms: In place of things, now the focus is on the *idea* of things. It is symptomatic that earlier, at the beginning, if two or three people from the charismatic renewal would find themselves together, they would start to pray; now, if two or three people in the renewal come together, most of the time they start talking about the importance of prayer! It seems like a small difference, but it is an enormous one; it is this difference that defines the renewal.

In this phase, a certain *ritualism* comes about: People do the same things that they did earlier, but without the power of the earlier days because the Spirit and life are lacking within. On both sides of the ocean, the same feeling of a certain weariness and burnout can be observed. At times I think that Mary observes our prayer meetings and turns to her Son and repeats, with a certain sadness, the same request made at Cana in Galilee: "They have no wine" (John 2:3b).

We have here a goal specifically indicated by these words from St. Paul: Strive to not end with the flesh; strive to give the power back to God again. Every incursion of the flesh that we can become aware of among us is not a defeat but a victory, because to expose enemies is already to have conquered them. This is a work of deliverance that the Word of God is accomplishing among us now.

One particular way of "ending with the flesh" is to focus on externals. By *externals* I do not quite mean raising or clapping our hands or the gestures that accompany our prayer when we are together. I mean instead an excessive preoccupation with our external image: What people say and think of us, or—a separate issue—making everything that the Lord is doing in everyone's hearts or in the group public (and doing it immediately), even when they are things that would be better kept hidden because they are "the secret of the king." At times we need to recall certain sayings from Jesus, such as "Sound no trumpet before you" (Matthew 6:2a) and "Do not let your left hand know what your right hand is doing" (Matthew 6:3). Making everything public (apart from the things that we can and should testify to for everyone's edification) puts the things of the Spirit in the same category as the seed that fell by the wayside: The birds came and carried it away. And we know who these birds are.

Many times this is dictated even by a good intention—the good intention of making ourselves known to the Church and of testifying about the wonders of the Lord. But here we are walking on a tightrope. The esteem and approval of the Church—the pope and the bishops—is a good thing, a gift from God. Indeed, we should desire to function in full communion with the Church and to walk on the right path. But too much of a *desire* and concern for this esteem and approval could cease being a good thing and become a bad thing, to become a matter of "seeking the favor of men" instead of God's favor. The apostle specifically reproves the Galatians for this (Galatians 1:10). The apostle also wrote to the Romans, "Would you have no fear of him who is in authority? Then do what is good, and you will receive his approval" (Romans 13:3). "Do what is good": This is all that concerns us. To be praised or not will follow of its own accord and does not depend on our seeking after it but on our "goodness"— that is, our orthodoxy, obedience, discipline, and humility. We should not want to see the smoke more than the fire that produces it; we have been called to be concerned about the "fire" in the Church, not the smoke—about God's glory, not ours! Let us remember these words of Jesus and make them ours: "Yet I do not seek my own glory; there is One who seeks it and he will be the judge": the Father (John 8:50).

Another way of "ending with the flesh" that threatens us is the temptation to want to do everything, to be a complete and total ecclesial force that embraces all camps and is present in all its sectors. There are brothers who, in good faith, would like the charismatic renewal to become involved with works of social justice, culture, volunteer work, education, youth, drug addicts, and so on. The past experience of the Church shows that this is usually the best way to flatten religious orders and to make them lose their particular charism and, therefore, also their original strength. In the end—as is partly the case today—everyone is doing the same things, and the contemplative orders are hardly distinguishable from the active orders. Wanting to do everything and to be everything is also a temptation to pride!

One day some "ministers" (that is, superiors), accompanied by a cardinal, came to Francis of Assisi, asking him to introduce into his Order of Friars Minor some norms from the Rules of St. Benedict, St. Augustine, and St. Bernard so that the life of the friars would be more "regulated" and their studies more serious. The *Poverello* took the cardinal by the hand, led him in front of the assembly of friars gathered there at the general chapter, and exclaimed:

My brothers, my brothers, God called me to walk in the way of humility and showed me the way of simplicity.... The

Lord has told me that he wanted to make a new fool of me in the world.... [To the visitors, he said,] God will use your personal knowledge and your wisdom to confound you.... Then to your shame you will return to your first state [your original vocation].[7]

St. Francis respected the other religious orders. They existed to accomplish certain important works, and he believed they should continue to do so, but he saw no reason to initiate a kind of competition.

Who knows if God isn't calling us, too, in the charismatic renewal to be "new fools" in the world, with that special kind of foolishness that Paul spoke about to the Corinthians: "We are fools for Christ's sake, but you are wise in Christ" (1 Corinthians 4:10a)?

Let us ask ourselves, then, "What is our charism?" What is the thing for which God has raised up the charismatic renewal? No one, I believe, doubts that we in this renewal "have begun in the Spirit," but in order to not "end with the flesh" we need to return to the One we began with, to return to the essential things, to return to the days of our youth, which are not so far off. Our vocation is to affirm through the Spirit the actual, present-day lordship of Jesus in the Church. It is "to give the power back to God" or to "Ascribe power to God" (Psalm 68:34a). It is simply to affirm that God is God. Children and poor people, like those who greeted Jesus when he made his entry into Jerusalem, are sufficient for that. But if no one declares these things, Jesus will be forced to make the stones cry out.

The Baptism in the Spirit

There are moments and actions in which this power of God is proclaimed with major purity: The outpouring of, or the baptism in, the Spirit! What have we done with this outpouring of the Spirit? The grace that is specific to the charismatic renewal is enclosed in it. Jesus appears there as the One who "is." He shows himself there as the Lord who gives the Spirit. There, a human being is nothing, and God is everything. If we could gather together the experiences of all the people involved, especially those who came at the beginning, we would discover how many lives this outpouring has renewed and how many vocations it has stirred up.

Now, however, the outpouring is considered by some to be secondary. We have groups in which few have received it and who believe that the outpouring is actually not so important for the charismatic renewal to continue. They keep saying, "But we have received baptism, and the Spirit was already given in baptism," and so on. Jesus was also full of the Spirit at his conception in Mary's womb, and yet he wanted to receive the baptism in Jordan, and all of the Spirit came on him once again. The reason is that for every new mission and vocation there corresponds a new outpouring of the Spirit. Only the first one is sacramental for us, but all the others are renewals of it, of the initial baptismal grace.

I am convinced that the weakening of the charismatic renewal begins with that kind of neglect; apart from the outpouring of the Spirit, the renewal does not differ greatly from today's other ecclesial movements. I feel impelled to repeat the words of Paul to the Galatians: "Did you experience so many things in vain?" (Galatians 3:4). We need to return to appreciating this gift more, to having good seminars and more outpourings. We need to wake up from Christian lives that are drowsy and exhausted. Once this happens, people could then be involved in everything, each one according to his or her disposition: social commitment, evangelism, religious vocations, etc. Then these would be expressions of the dynamism of the Spirit and not merely forms of human activity. St. Francis was urged to obtain a papal privilege to preach and hear confessions in various churches (since the prelates often denied permission for it). He answered, "This concern should not be yours, because if sinners are converted they will find many confessors."[8] Likewise we should be concerned above all with conversion, with awakening faith in people, knowing that they will then find in the Church all that they need to nourish their newfound life again.

We should have the desire in our hearts that the charismatic renewal be, or return to being, the place in which the Risen One can proclaim his uncontested "I AM"! We should want him to be able to look at us and surround us with his gaze and with the arms of the Pantokrator (like the Christ in the Romanesque cathedral in Monreale, Italy) and to say with joy, "Here I AM, and there is no other!" We should have a desire that he see all the smoldering lights of our extinguished "I"s waiting for the One who is "the radiant Star of the morning," the Sun of righteousness returned alive from hell. We should have a desire that the words we heard at the beginning—"The Lord alone will be exalted in that day!"—would come to pass among us.

Oh, Lord Jesus, king of glory, radiant bridegroom of the Church, we have indeed lifted you up on the cross, and now we know who YOU ARE. Be, Lord Jesus! Be in me, in my group, in the charismatic renewal, in the Church. We rejoice that the Father has given you that name, and at your name we bow down in adoration. Amen!

CHAPTER THREE

From the Old Man to the New Man

If we compare the New Testament texts on putting off the old man and clothing ourselves with the new, we see a peculiar oscillation. The apostle says in one place, "Put off the old man that belongs to your former manner of life and is corrupt through deceitful lusts, and be renewed in the spirit of your minds, and put on the new man, created after the likeness of God in true righteousness and holiness" (Ephesians 4:22–24). Here, putting away the old man and being clothed with the new man is a command, something that lies before us and that we need to accomplish in our lives. However, in a different text from the apostle, we see that everything is presented instead as something that has already happened and that lies behind us: "You have put off the old man with his practices and have put on the new man, who is being renewed in knowledge after the image of his creator" (Colossians 3:9–10).

The same oscillation is repeated when it concerns "putting on Christ." At times it is a command, something we need to do: "Put on the Lord Jesus Christ" (Romans 13:14a). At other times it is presented as something that has already happened through baptism: "As many of you as were baptized into Christ have put on Christ" (Galatians 3:27).

What does this seemingly opposite-sounding series of expressions mean? Is the word of God perhaps contradicting itself? On the contrary, it is only a seeming contradiction that contains a fundamental insight into the issue. Scripture is telling us that the transition from the old man to the new man is both our work *and* the work of God, a work still to be accomplished *and* a work accomplished already.

Prior to any decision or effort for self-discipline on our part, the creation of the new nature is a great event that has already been accomplished historically, and its effect has reached each of us individually in baptism. Prior to being our work, it was a work of God. It coincides with the transition from the old to the new covenant, from the letter to the Spirit, from law to grace. We need to discover what we have become in baptism in order to understand what we ought to do in life. Our duty flows out of who we have become: "If we live by the Spirit, let us also walk by the Spirit" (Galatians 5:25).

This is something that the charismatic renewal contributes and that is very new and useful: It helps believers rediscover not only who they are but also the divine reality that they bear within themselves. This discovery enables them to accomplish what the gospel asks of them more easily and to do it not out of a sense of obligation but out of gratitude, not out of fear but out of love.

Although I could address this topic in a special way to young people, it essentially concerns each of us and should help reveal the potential for light, newness, and hope that the charismatic renewal holds for us. It can point willing hearts to spiritual goals. I do not mean here the charismatic renewal as a movement but rather the Holy Spirit, whom the renewal wants to help others rediscover.

The charismatic renewal does not present itself as an alternative in this regard, much less as in opposition to or in competition with other ecclesial groups. Its goal is not to outline programs for living out the faith and translate that faith into particular activities on a cultural and political plane. Instead, the role of the charismatic renewal is to indicate where people can find the power to accomplish all those other activities—namely, the Holy Spirit. The renewal's contribution, then, is humble, and in a certain sense the humblest one there is, because it has nothing to offer on its own, nothing that is the fruit of its own discernment, invention, or programming. What it proposes belongs to all Christians in the same way; everyone possesses it. It is the original Christian "given" that precedes its diverse expressions and specific embodiments throughout history. Because of this, it is "of value in every way," just as godliness is (see 1 Timothy 4:8). It is not even a movement in the same way that other movements are; it does not, in fact, have founders or theoreticians. And it should not have any. The charismatic renewal, therefore, esteems and is grateful to the brothers and sisters who assume the difficult burden of taking the next step and pointing out working models that can translate faith into different situations in life.

The apostle John, in his First Letter, says, "I write to you, young men, because you are strong, and the word of God abides in you, and you have overcome the Evil One" (1 John 2:14b). I can paraphrase these words and say, "'Little children, you are of God, and have overcome them; for he who is in you is greater than he who is in the world' (1 John 4:4). I exhort you to become stronger, and I remind you that you are new men and women, and I exhort you to be even more so."

In line with the above premises, this teaching is divided into two parts. In the first part I will deal with the transition from the old man to the new man insofar as it is a work of God already accomplished. In the second part I will deal with the transition from the old man to the new man insofar as it is our work, always needing to be accomplished anew.

From the Old Man to the New Man: An Accomplished Work

The theme of the transition from the old man to the new or, in other words, from living in the flesh to living in the Spirit is unfolded by St. Paul especially in the text of Romans 8:1–13. It begins: "There is therefore now no condemnation for those who are in Christ Jesus. For the law of the Spirit of life in Christ Jesus has set me free from the law of sin and death" (Romans 8:1–2). All of what Paul says here about the Spirit is presented as a counterpoint to what he has just said about the law. Even the Spirit himself is described as law: "The law of the Spirit" means, in fact, "the law which is the Spirit."

This is surprising to us because if there are two things that are mutually exclusive in everyone's mind, they are precisely the Spirit and the law. Even if people can sometimes speak about the "spirit of the law," they cannot then invert that and speak about a "law of the Spirit." However, it is different with the Bible, which indeed can speak of the "law of the Spirit." To be convinced of that we need only go back to the coming of the Spirit, to Pentecost.

In the Old Testament there are two basic interpretations of the feast of Pentecost. At the beginning, Pentecost was the "festival of the seven weeks" (Tobit 2:1) or the "feast of weeks" (Numbers 28:26), when the first fruits were offered to God (see Exodus 23:16; Deuteronomy 16:9). After that, however, at the time of Jesus, the feast was enriched with new significance. It was the feast of the covenant and the giving of the law on Sinai. It was the feast, in short, that commemorated the events narrated in Exodus 19—20. According to the Bible's calculations, the law was given on Sinai fifty days after the celebration of the Passover and the exodus from Egypt. On Sinai, God gave Moses the law, the Decalogue, establishing a covenant with his people, thus making them "a kingdom of priests and a holy nation" (Exodus 19:4–6). It seems that Luke in Acts, describing the coming of the Holy Spirit on the apostles, deliberately described it in terms that recalled the theophany on Sinai.

What does this parallel to our Pentecost tell us? In other words, what does it mean that the Holy Spirit came upon the Church on the very day that Israel was commemorating the giving of the law and the covenant? At this point the answer is clear: It is to indicate that the

Holy Spirit is the new law, the spiritual law that seals the new and everlasting covenant and consecrates a new royal and priestly people, which is the Church. What a wonderful revelation about the meaning of Pentecost and about the Holy Spirit himself! This immediately clarifies the prophecies of Jeremiah and of Ezekiel concerning the new covenant: "This is the covenant which I will make with the house of Israel after those days, says the LORD: I will put my law within them, and I will write it upon their hearts" (Jeremiah 31:33a). It is no longer written on tablets of stone but on hearts; it is no longer an external law but an internal law. Ezekiel specifies what this internal law consists of: "A new heart I will give you, and a new spirit I will put within you…. I will put my spirit within you" (Ezekiel 36:26–27a). The new law is the "new spirit," the Holy Spirit.

St. Paul clearly alludes to the fulfillment of these prophecies when he calls the community of the new covenant "a letter from Christ,… written not with ink but with the Spirit of the living God, not on tablets of stone but on tablets of human hearts" (2 Corinthians 3:3).

The Letter and Grace

The big difference between the two laws, says the apostle, is that the new law gives life while the old law does not: "For the law of the Spirit of life in Christ Jesus has set me free from the law of sin and death" (Romans 8:2). Since the Mosaic law is a norm that is external to human beings, that law—and, with it, every positive law—does not change people's inner condition. It does not take away sin but reveals it; it does not give life but only brings to light the death that exists in people.

The reason is that sin, beginning with Adam's sin, consists in human beings wanting to be like God, in believing that they can exist without God. Sin does not come from the transgression of the law; rather, the transgression of the law comes from sin. Original sin is present prior to the actual transgression of the divine precept; it consists in being alienated from God and in setting oneself in opposition to him internally. Disobedience to the law of not eating from the tree is the manifestation, or effect, of this internal opposition to God, just as, up to that point, the observance of the law not to eat of the tree was the effect rather than the cause of friendship with God. Life and death come before the law—whether it be observed or transgressed. Life and death reflect something that happens in the depths of the human heart.

That is why the fundamental sin, the love of self rather than of God, cannot be removed by the law; it can be removed only when that original state of friendship—which the serpent induced Adam and Eve to destroy through envy—can be reestablished. And that is precisely what occurred in the redemption through Christ: "For God has done what the law, weakened by the flesh, could not do…[by] sending his own Son" (Romans 8:3). Jesus, because of his death and resurrection, gave us his Spirit at Pentecost and, in a particular way, in baptism—the same Holy Spirit that he had. When the Spirit comes to people, he changes their inner condition. As long as people want to be like God and to live under the rule of sin, God will inevitably appear to them as the adversary, as the obstacle. There is deep-seated hostility between ourselves and God, which the law merely brings to light. Egotistical human beings "lust after," or desire, certain things, and God is the one who blocks their path through his commandments, opposing them in their desires with his "You should…. You should not!" Paul says that, "the mind that is set on the flesh is hostile to God; it does not submit to God's law, indeed it cannot" (Romans 8:7).

Under grace, God ceases being "the other," the obstacle. This is not because we have changed our innate tendency (not by works!) but because God draws near to us and removes the hostility, on his own initiative, through the blood of Christ. Here, then, is the new thing brought by the Spirit at Pentecost: Even while we had a deep-seated rancor in the depths of our hearts against God, the Holy Spirit came to us on God's behalf and created in each of us a new person who loves God and freely does the things he commands. The Spirit, in fact, witnesses to us that God is favorable toward us and that he is our ally, not our enemy. He makes us see all that God the Father is able to do for us in Christ and to see that he did not spare even his own Son for us. In short, he conquers our hearts in such a way that we can now freely do all that he commands us.

God, however, does not limit himself to commanding us to do or not do this or that, but he himself performs with us and within us the things that are commanded. The law that is the Spirit, then, is far more than an order or a commandment; it is a living, active principle. The Spirit is the new law and the new life. Because of this, the new law is most often simply called grace: "You are not under law but under grace" (Romans 6:14b; see John 1:17). Jesus defines his law in contrast to the Mosaic law. He defines it as an easy yoke and a light burden (see Matthew 11:30), but it is not because it is less rigorous than the Mosaic law—it is incomparably more so!—but because it is not a yoke and a burden that we must carry alone.

The New Commandment

But how, concretely, does this new law of the Spirit work? It works through love! We could say that the new law is nothing other than what Jesus called the new commandment. The Holy Spirit has written the new law in our hearts, infusing them with love. In fact, the Bible says, "God's love has been poured into our hearts through the Holy Spirit who has been given to us" (Romans 5:5b). This not only speaks of the love with which God loves us but also of the love with which God makes it possible for us to love him and our neighbor. It is a new ability to love. Love is the sign and the proof of the new life of the Spirit: "We know," writes St. John, "that we have passed out of death into life, because we love the brethren" (1 John 3:14a).

Jesus called love the new commandment, even though it already existed in the Old Testament, because love was formerly only one commandment among many; it was only one part of the old law. The innovation consists in love now being no longer one commandment among many but in love being *the* commandment. It is not only the object of love that has changed (broadened, in fact, to embrace all men and women and not just one's countrymen and friends), but its very nature has also changed. It is no longer a love acquired through one's own efforts but a love infused in us freely by God. It is no longer the letter but the Spirit.

If Jesus had limited himself to proclaiming the new commandment, saying, "A new commandment I give to you, that you love one another" (John 13:34a), it would have remained an old law, as it was earlier. However, when at Pentecost he poured that love into the hearts of his disciples by means of the Spirit, it became the new law, the law of the Spirit who gives life. Now the commandment is doubly new—not only because it is new but also because it makes us new, not only in the passive but in the active sense. St. Augustine exclaims, "This love renews us that we may be new men, heirs of the New Testament.... Even now it also renews the nations, and from the whole human race, which is scattered over the whole world, it makes and gathers a new people, the body of the new spouse, the bride of the Son of God, the Only-Begotten."[9]

Anyone who approaches the gospel with a secular mentality would find it strange that love is made a "commandment." What kind of love is it, one would ask, if it is not free but commanded? To answer this objection we need to know that there are two ways in which people can be induced to do, or not do, a certain thing: either through constraint or through attraction. The law induces them through constraint, with the threat of punishment; love induces them through attraction. Without having to experience any constraints, people are attracted by what they love. Love is like a force of gravity in the soul, drawing it toward the object of its desire, where it is sure of finding rest.

In this sense, love is a law, a commandment: It creates in Christians a dynamic that leads us to do all that God wants, spontaneously, without even having to think about it, because, by this time, we have made God's will ours and we love everything that God loves. Love adheres to the will of God in its essence before it is codified into law and written proscriptions. It attains, through the Spirit, the living and holy will of God.

However, it is also the most compelling law there is, because it impels us to do things that are so arduous that no written law could ever succeed in making us do them merely with the threat of punishment:

> The lover flies, runs and rejoices; he is free and nothing can restrain him.... Love often knows no measure, but burns beyond measure. Love feels no burden, values no labours, would like to do more than it can do, without pleading impossibility, because it believes that it may and can do all things. In fact, it is ready to do anything, and it performs and effects many things, in which he who does not love faints and succumbs.[10]

This is the way it happens when a young man and a young woman are in love. How much more so, then, if we are in love with God?

From the Old Man to the New Man: A Transition to Be Accomplished

Many, after hearing about this new existence that is brought forth by the Spirit and based on love, have perhaps become attracted to it. This is precisely what the word of God seeks to accomplish: to stir up in us an ardent desire to belong to this new world. Alongside this desire, however, a sense of skepticism and discouragement can also arise. Someone might ask, "Where is this freedom, this capacity to love and to follow the commandments? Where is this new life? Is this only a lovely but abstract theory? And why do some people achieve this new life and this liberty while others do not?"

St. Paul answers all these questions in only a few words in the following part of his text: "If by the Spirit you put to death the deeds of the body you will live" (Romans 8:13b). The key is articulated here: putting to death, mortification. There is only one bridge from the old man to the new man, and that bridge is mortification. This is where our part begins. The apostle told us at the beginning of his text that the Spirit "gives life"; now at the end, he tells us that the Spirit gives it through our "putting to death the deeds of the body." Baptism has made us new human beings, but this newness, if it is to continue, needs to be renewed from day to day (see 2 Corinthians 4:16). "This newness," wrote Origen, "must, if it can be said, be renewed" (*Ipsa novitas innovanda est*).[11] Mortifying the old nature is the condition for this continuous renewal.

The Spirit, then, gives life, but he gives it through death. Just like what happened to Jesus! He was "put to death in the flesh," and because of that God made him "alive in the spirit" (1 Peter 3:18). The real new man is Jesus. We cannot succeed in becoming new men and women unless we are "becoming like him in his death" (Philippians 3:10): "If we have died with him, we shall also live with him" (2 Timothy 2:11).

When we speak of new life in the Spirit, we always run the risk of understanding this expression in a human way. We can think it is an empowering and a development of our former life, or an answer to our natural need and instinct to live, or a new wave of energy that pleasantly permeates body and soul. Instead, new life means something completely different and more radical; it literally means a new life, a life that begins all over again, after the occurrence of a death. The road a traveler begins on can be "new" in two ways: either the road he was following earlier has been refurbished (has new asphalt or has been made straight), or the road he was following earlier came to an intersection and he turned onto another road. The new life in the Spirit is new in this second sense.

We need to look at mortification in a new light to understand that we do not need to fear it. Jesus said once, "I am the true vine, and my Father is the vinedresser. Every branch of mine that bears no fruit, he takes away, and every branch that does bear fruit he prunes, that it may bear more fruit" (John 15:1–2). Mortification has the same function as pruning. In baptism, a seed of new life was grafted into us. If we look at what happens in agriculture when a grafting occurs, we see that the rest of the tree is allowed to exist for a little while so that the old and the new do not both die. But once the grafting has taken hold and the first buds have come forth, the farmer cuts and prunes all the branches of the old tree one by one. Otherwise, all the strength of the tree would be absorbed by those old branches and would produce only the wild fruit it used to produce.

In the same way, the old tree, the old man, remains in us after baptism. Its branches are the different passions, and its wild fruit consists of the works of the flesh. The apostle elsewhere gives us a list of what these fruits of the flesh are: "immorality, impurity, licentiousness, idolatry, sorcery, enmity, strife, jealousy, anger, selfishness, dissension, party spirit, envy, drunkenness, carousing, and the like" (Galatians 5:19–21).

Holiness, like sculpture, is achieved by "the art of removing," that is, by eliminating the useless parts. There is a story that one day Michelangelo, walking in a courtyard in Florence, saw a block of rough marble covered with dust and mud. He stopped abruptly to look at it, and then, as though inspecting it with an invisible lamp, he said to those present, "There is an angel hidden in that block of stone; I want to bring him forth!" And he began to work with his chisel to give shape to the angel he had dimly glimpsed.

It is the same with us. We are still great blocks of rough stone covered with a lot of "dust" and have many useless parts. God the Father looks at us and says, "The image of my Son is hidden in this piece of stone; I want to bring it forth so that it can shine next to me in heaven for all eternity!" If from now on we feel the blows of a chisel and we see parts of ourselves fall to the ground, let us not misunderstand any longer. We should not continue to ask, "What have I done wrong? Why is God punishing me this way?" Let us endeavor to say to ourselves, instead, "God loves me and wants to form in me the image of his Jesus. Endure it, my soul!" The cross is the chisel with which God shapes his chosen ones. This has always been the case.

The most open-hearted souls not only withstand the blows of the chisel that come from outside, but they also collaborate with them as much as possible, freely imposing on themselves small or large acts of mortification and breaking their old will. According to one of the Desert Fathers,

> if...we desire to be set free and to enjoy perfect freedom, let us learn to cut off our desires, and so, with God's help in a little while, we shall make progress and arrive at a state of tranquility.... In a short time a man can cut off ten...desires. He takes a little walk and sees something. His thoughts say to him, "Go over there and investigate," and he says to his thoughts, "No! I won't," and he cuts off his desire.[12]

This Desert Father draws examples from the monastic life, but they are easy to adapt to other stations in life. There is an unhealthy show on television, a provocative poster on a wall, or a pornographic magazine within reach. The man with the old nature says, "Look!" and instantly offers you a hundred pretexts and excuses for you to do it. But you answer, "No!" and you break your will. Some friends are gossiping and are saying bad things about someone; your old man says, "Join in; tell them what you know." But you reply, "No!" and you put to death the old man. You pass by a young man or woman you do not like and who does not like you and who is unpleasant to you; your pride says, "Keep to yourself and don't speak!" But instead you smile, you greet him or her, and you conquer yourself, breaking your pride. You meet a poor person, perhaps a foreigner, who you know will ask you for something. You want to pull back or cross the street, but instead you go toward that person out of love for Jesus: You have made your new man win.

Today, people are summoned to many noble battles on every side: the war against drugs, hunger, injustice, pollution, war itself. Jesus summons us to a warfare that is different from the others and without which the others are only palliatives: the war against one's "I," against the man with the old nature, against oneself.

In baptism and in confirmation (and then in the outpouring of the Spirit that has renewed these sacraments in many of us), we were consecrated as soldiers for Christ. But we must not fool ourselves. This is the war above all others for which we were made soldiers: "Take your suffering as a good soldier of Christ Jesus" (2 Timothy 2:3).

We must do whatever is needed to redeem the word "mortification" from the suspicion that hovers over it. People today, yielding to the demands of the old man without realizing it, have created a special philosophy to justify and even exalt the satisfaction of their own instincts, or, as people say, of their own natural impulses, thinking that this is the road to self-fulfillment. As if people needed the incentive of such a philosophy! Isn't our corrupt human nature, our egotism, already enough?

However, mortification is done in vain and becomes a "work of the flesh" if it is done for its own sake, without freedom, or, worse, if it is done in order to make claims on God or to elicit praise from men. This is, unfortunately, how many Christians have perceived mortification, and now, having tasted the freedom of the Spirit, they are afraid to fall back into it. But there is a different way of understanding mortification, one that comes from the word of God, an entirely spiritual and charismatic way because it comes from the Spirit: "If by the Spirit you put to death the deeds of the body you will live." This kind of mortification is a fruit of the Spirit and brings forth life.

St. Francis of Assisi reconciled the men of his time with poverty, which was abhorred by all, by presenting it lovingly to the world as a great lady, as "Lady Poverty." I would like to do the same with mortification. I present her to myself first, and then to you, like the bride of the Spirit, as the one who unites herself to the Spirit to give us life: "Lady Mortification!" Mortification guards and preserves love.

According to Søren Kierkegaard,

> If a man honestly says: God is love, then this man *eo ipso* has only one desire, to love God (who is love) with all of his heart and all his strength. And when God discovers that this is the way it is with a man, that he has this desire, God says: Yes, yes, my dear child, if this is the case, I shall help you, I shall help you to die to the world, for otherwise you cannot love me.—Take a purely human relationship. If the lover is not able to speak the beloved's language, he or she must learn it, however difficult it may seem to them—otherwise, if they cannot talk together, there cannot be a happy relationship. It is the same with dying to the world in order to be able to love God. God is spirit—only one who has died to the world can speak this language at all. If you do not wish to die to the world, then you cannot love God either; you are talking about entirely different matters than he is.[13]

"Take My Yoke Upon You!"

I would now like to talk about the call that follows from everything we have heard. It is Jesus himself who presents this call to us from the Gospel, saying, "Take my yoke upon you" (Matthew 11:29a). The image of a yoke is often used in the Bible to symbolize the law. The new law of Christ, the law of the Spirit, is also a yoke, something that entails a sacrifice for fallen humanity, something that "weighs" on the old man because it calls for mortification, self-denial. But it is an "easy" yoke, a "light" weight. What is it that makes this yoke easy, likable, and desirable? What is it that has always set the saints and generous souls on fire to accept this yoke of mortification, and even to seek it out, until they could not live without it? The reason is that this yoke is the yoke of love, the yoke that joins a person to the beloved. In a work from the second century, written in the style of the Psalms, these marvelous words are put into Christ's mouth: "I lifted up over them the yoke of my love; like the arm of the bridegroom over the bride, so was my yoke over those that know me."[14]

Yes, mortification is the yoke that keeps us united to God. Jesus put himself under the yoke of the cross first, and, even though he is resurrected, that is where he still is. He waits there for whoever wishes to come alongside him and take up the other end of the yoke, he waits there for the person who will accept the arm of the bridegroom around his or her shoulder.

Mortification keeps us united not only to Christ but also to one another; it is the way to have unity with brothers and sisters. The extent to which we give ourselves to our brothers and sisters is the extent to which we are disposed to deny ourselves. To please our neighbor, we need to renounce always wanting to please ourselves (see Romans 15:1–2). For this reason, the more that the "I" is mortified, the more that unity will flourish within groups, parishes, and the church.

Mortification especially keeps a man and a woman united in marriage. In fact, it cuts egotism in half, that stubborn self-affirmation that is the chief enemy. In marriage, mortification preserves love. It teaches couples to hold back hurtful words that cause bitterness and coldness and to speak only words that are good and that lead to mutual charity and edification (see Ephesians 4:29).

Spouses can be described as "conjoined" (in Latin, *coniuges*), which etymologically means "united under the same yoke." If that yoke is the yoke of the flesh, of pleasure, or only of duty, it very soon becomes heavy and unbearable. Jesus offers Christian spouses who live in the Spirit the possibility of becoming "conjoined" in an altogether different sense: They are "conjoined" because they are under the same yoke, Christ's yoke, which is the yoke of love. He says to them, in a special way, "Take my yoke upon you, and learn from me; for I am gentle and lowly in heart, and you will find rest for your souls" (Matthew 11:29).

You will find rest! This is why St. Paul exhorts those who marry to do so "in the Lord" (see 1 Corinthians 7:39). To marry in the Lord means far more than simply being married in the Church; it means putting the marriage under the lordship of Christ, entrusting a decision made in time to something that really belongs to eternity. If you marry relying only on your own feelings or on the enthusiasm of a love in the budding stage, when that initial love diminishes you will find yourselves faced with the obligation of loving forever, and duty all by itself will not be enough to sustain love. But if, on the other hand, you place your marriage relationship under the shelter of grace, if you have built on the rock that does not change, then you can always return to it again to find grace, finding the foundation for unity there every time. The words of the prophet Zechariah are also relevant for those who marry: "Not by might, nor by power, but by my Spirit, says the LORD of hosts" (Zechariah 4:6b).

From new men and women, then, new families are born spontaneously. But new priests are also born, and this is the last call I ask you to hear, the call of religious vocation. St. Paul speaks of a service in the Spirit (*diakonia Pneumatos*) that specifically concerns ministers of the New Testament (see 2 Corinthians 3:8). This service is usually explained as priesthood and consecrated life. The Church never loses an occasion to address young people, saying, "Come! There is a need for you. The harvest is abundant, but the laborers are few and becoming fewer."

Isn't this a calling, a vocation? Too often people worry for years, searching within themselves for who knows what signs to recognize their vocation. But isn't that a sign in itself? God is calling today through the Church; that voice is also God's voice. "Today, when you hear his voice, / do not harden your hearts" (Hebrews 3:7). It is a good thing to have a family, but it is even better to make a commitment to gathering together and serving the family of God. Save your lives by losing them. Do not let yourselves be discouraged by our mediocrity; new priests in a new Church can be—and will be—better priests than we were.

The two vocations—marriage and consecrated life—come from the same Spirit; each has its own charism (see 1 Corinthians 7:7). As with every charism, each not only serves the individual but is also "for the common good." A new unity and complementarity are coming forth among the people of God between married and consecrated people for their mutual edification. Married couples are a sign and a gift for priests, and religious are a sign and a gift for married people. Each group senses a need for the other.

There are countries and cultures in the non-Christian world (but sometimes, unfortunately, also in the Christian world) where the relationship between the priest and the people is still based on a rigid separation between the sacred and the secular. The priest prays, fulfills rites, and performs sacrifices for the people and ministers the things of God to them; the people provide the priest with worldly goods. I recently observed this during a trip to the Orient, and I was quite struck by it. The religious piety of the people in the village expressed itself every morning by their filling up the bowl of the holy man who then prayed and meditated on their behalf.

We cannot content ourselves with the kind of relationship that reduces the laity to serving only through material and worldly goods. They too live "in the Spirit" and have their own spiritual gifts with which they sanctify the people of God, according to an excerpt in a document from the Second Vatican Council.[15] The Spirit teaches a very different kind of relationship among us. It is true that laypeople contribute to the support of the clergy, but their contribution to the kingdom and to the priests should not stop there. The Lord today is calling the faithful in ever-growing numbers to pray, to offer sacrifices, in order to have holy priests. A concern, a passion, for holy priests has spread as a sign of the times throughout today's Church. Mother Teresa of Calcutta continued to repeat this need. Having heard the cry of the poor of the world, whenever she found herself addressing priests she conveyed that cry (as she did once before the synod of bishops), saying, "They told me to tell you that they need holy priests."[16]

The royal and universal priesthood of believers has found a new way of expressing itself: contributing to the sanctification of ministerial priesthood. Such vocations are extending out more and more beyond the walls of the cloistered monasteries, where they have been hidden, and are reaching the faithful. This vocation is becoming widespread, a call that God addresses to many. Through prayer, people are supporting the proclamation of the word and increasing its effectiveness and its fruitfulness. I share with you my time, my study, and the understanding that I acquired from the treasure house of the Church, but others, who are unknown, have contributed the most precious thing: prayer and suffering. Therefore, I cannot boast about myself, and if I do I am a thief and a usurper.

God calls some souls to the even higher task of atoning for priests. One day Jesus said to one of these (an extraordinary mother of a Mexican family who died in 1937 and for whom the process of canonization has been initiated):

This will truly be a solace to My heart, giving Me holy priests. Tell Me you accept, that you will belong with Me to priests always, since your mission on behalf of them will continue in heaven. Yet here you have another martyrdom. What priests will do against Me, you will feel, since it is in this that basically associating yourself to My priesthood consists, in that you feel and you suffer because of their unfaithfulness and wretchedness. In this way you glorify the Trinity. We will have the same reasons for suffering.[17]

"The male is a priest," wrote Paul Claudel, "but it is not forbidden a woman to be [a sacrificial] victim."[18] Only men can be priests, but the wisdom of God has kept aside a task for women, an even higher task in a certain sense, which the world does not understand and thus rejects with disdain: that of forming priests and of contributing to raising the quality, not the quantity, of Catholic priesthood.

I end with these vibrant words from St. Augustine that make the best comment on our theme:

My brothers and sisters, my children, O seedlings of the Catholic Church, O holy and heavenly seed, O you that have been born again in Christ and been born from above, listen to me—or rather, listen to God through me: *Sing to the Lord a new song* (Ps 149:1).[19]

Sing him a new song. Strip off your oldness, you know a new song. A new person, a New Covenant, a new song. People stuck in the old life have no business with this new song; only they can learn it who are new persons, renewed by grace and throwing off the old, sharers already in the New Covenant, which is the kingdom of heaven.... Let us sing this new song not with our tongues but with our lives.... Sing to him *in jubilation*.... But what is that? It is to grasp the fact that what is sung in the heart cannot be articulated in words. Think of people who sing at harvest time, or in the vineyard, or at any work that goes with a swing. They begin by caroling their joy in words, but after a while they seem to be so full of gladness that they find words no longer adequate to express it, so they abandon distinct syllables and words, and resort to a single cry of jubilant happiness. Jubilation is a shout of joy; it indicates that the heart is bringing forth what defies speech. To whom, then, is this jubilation more fittingly offered than to God who surpasses all utterance? You cannot speak of him because he transcends our speech; and if you cannot speak of him, yet may not remain silent, what else can you do but cry out in jubilation...? *Sing skillfully to him in jubilation.*[20]

All that remains now is to sing in tongues.

CHAPTER FOUR

"Eternity! Eternity!"

In the book of Numbers we read about the incident in which God commanded Moses to gather seventy men together in the tent of meeting. When they were assembled, God caused his Spirit to rest on them, and they began to prophesy. However, at the same time, in another part of the camp, the Spirit of God also came upon two men, Eldad and Medad, even though they were not with Moses in the tent of meeting, and they also began to prophesy. Young Joshua ran to Moses and reported to him what was happening outside the tent and asked him to stop it, but Moses answered, "Are you jealous for my sake? Would that all the LORD's people were prophets, that the LORD would put his spirit upon them!" (Numbers 11:29).

Moses' wish came true on the day of Pentecost, when God poured out his Spirit on everyone and they began to proclaim in tongues the Lord's wonderful deeds. Moses' wish has come true again today in the Church, because since the Second Vatican Council we are experiencing a new Pentecost. The Lord is again giving his Spirit so that all of his people can become prophets capable of proclaiming his words and his mighty works.

"Come to Me, All Who Labor and Are Heavy Laden"

In this saying from Jesus we can distinguish four elements: an invitation, a promise, a condition, and an assurance.

It contains a universal *invitation:* Come to me *all* of you. There is no distinction here between young and old, rich and poor, believers and nonbelievers, righteous and sinners. All! Only one category of people is excluded: those who are neither weary nor oppressed, those who believe that they are enough in themselves, the "self-sufficient," those whom Mary in the Magnificat calls the "rich," who are sent away empty.

There is an equally universal *promise:* I will give you rest; I will heal you. He does not say, "I will heal some of you." No, he says, "I will heal all those of you who come to me." Neither does he say, "I will heal you of some things but not of others." He heals the whole person, and he heals all men and women; he is the physician of the body and of the soul. If anyone else in the world had made a promise of this kind, it goes without saying that he would be a presumptuous person or a charlatan. The world, especially in the large cities, is full of these kinds of charlatans and would-be wizards. Their publicity claims, "Come and find the solution for all your problems: health, finances, and love. Satisfaction guaranteed or your money back." But it is all just a hoax to siphon off money from naïve people—and when it is not just a clever hoax, it is something worse.

But in our case, it is Christ, the Son of God, who has said these things, the One to whom all things have been given by the Father (see Matthew 11:27). The best guarantee of the truth of his promise is that it has already been perfectly kept. In fact, Peter says of him in the Acts of the Apostles, "he went about doing good and healing all" (10:38).

There is, however, a *condition*, a demand: "Take my yoke upon you, and learn from me; for I am gentle and lowly in heart." What Jesus calls "my yoke" is first of all the one that he took upon himself. The yoke is the yoke of obedience. Taking up this yoke means saying to the Father, as Jesus said at Gethsemane, "May your will be done!" (see Matthew 26:39). "Take my yoke upon you": This is similar to another of Jesus' sayings: "If any man would come after me, let him deny himself and take up his cross and follow me" (Mark 8:34).

Finally, *assurance*: "You will find rest.... My yoke is easy, and my burden is light." There is a mystery here, a paradox: humbling oneself under the mighty hand of God, accepting his will, taking up one's cross—all of this produces an effect that is the opposite of the one we would expect. We are seeing a miracle, an unheard-of transformation. Things are exchanging nature and names: Weariness becomes refreshment, the yoke becomes ease, the burden becomes rest.

We need to discover the secret of this transformation. It involves making a leap that is almost infinite, which is usually called conversion. Only he who takes this leap will find rest and will go home with his burden "lightened." We come to Jesus wanting a certain thing, a grace, for example, or a healing. Instead, Jesus keeps in reserve for us something that is infinitely more important and more beautiful, something over and above the small thing we had in mind.

How will Jesus make us understand and accept this exchange? He could immediately give us the thing we are asking for; that would be easy for him. Jesus said to the Pharisees one day, "Which is easier, to say, 'Your sins are forgiven,' or to say, 'Rise and walk'?" (Matthew 9:5). It is easier for God to say, "Rise and walk!" because that costs him exactly nothing; he does not need to take into account our dreadful freedom. But in so doing, he knows that it would not be for our good and would harm us. He would be like a doctor whom we consulted about a cold and who, noticing that we had a tumor, simply cured our cold without doing anything for the tumor or even warning us about it.

We are instructed by the word of God to accept the glad exchange without murmuring against him. We are to obey this saying of Christ: "seek first his kingdom and his righteousness, and all these things shall be yours as well" (Matthew 6:33).

Living Water and Living Bread

There are two Gospel events that will help us understand the "leap" we need to make, the conversion we must undergo.

The first is the one we read about in the fourth chapter of the Gospel of John. The Samaritan woman, learning that Jesus had some kind of special water to give, immediately asked him, "'Sir, give me this water, that I may not thirst, nor come here to draw'" (John 4:15). Similarly, discovering that Jesus gives grace, we immediately rush to ask him, "Lord, give me this grace! Let me see, so that I don't have to depend on others anymore; let me walk so that I can go wherever I want; help my son find work or to graduate so that I, I, I..."

Pay close attention: Jesus does not disdain these requests. On the contrary, he is moved with compassion and even weeps over them. He cannot, however, leave us in this state of being prisoners of our "I." He must help us move on from this state in which we think only of ourselves and our own blessings down here. He cannot remove the mote from our eye and leave the beam.

Let us hear, then, what he answered the Samaritan woman on that occasion: "If you knew the gift of God...you would have asked...[for] living water" (John 4:10). Living water—Jesus has and wants to give a different kind of water, the water that makes a person no longer thirsty and that holds the definitive solution to the problem of thirst. This is the water that becomes "a spring of water welling up to eternal life" (John 4:14b). (The word "eternal" will be useful in what follows.)

It seems the woman made the right choice, because she immediately ran to her village, shouting out to all, "Come!" (John 4:29). Jesus had clearly said, in effect, "I am He, the one who is speaking to you: the Messiah, the living water, eternal life—it is I who speak to you" (see John 4:26). What a glad exchange! The woman came seeking water at the well and found God! Happy are those who seek healing and find God! Happy are those who want health and find salvation!

Let us move on to the second event, in John 6. First the discussion was about water. Now it is about bread. Shortly before, Jesus had multiplied the loaves and the fishes, and all the people had been satisfied; then he drew apart. But the report of it spread, and a group of people tracked him down on the other side of the lake in the synagogue at Capernaum.

They begin with an innocuous-sounding question but one that conceals a hidden agenda: "'Rabbi, when did you come here?'" (John 6:25b). Jesus, who sees into the heart, goes straight to the problem. He says to them, "You are not looking for me because of the sign but because you ate those loaves and want to eat them again. You are not looking for the reality behind that sign." Jesus begins to speak of his bread, and then they immediately say, like the Samaritan woman, "Lord, give us this bread always" (John 6:34). But Jesus was speaking of another bread, the bread that forever removes "hunger" from the person who eats it, the bread "which endures to eternal life" (Or "for eternity"—again that word! See John 6:26–27). And then the clear revelation comes: "'I am the bread of life; he who comes to me shall not hunger'" (John 6:35). Once again a choice, a leap.

This group of people needed to choose whether they would insist on wanting the bread that perishes, even though it was miraculously obtained, or whether they would receive the bread that never perishes—Jesus himself. We know how it ended. Some began to murmur among themselves, saying, "'This is a hard saying; who can listen to it?'" (John 6:60), and they went away. Others, on the other hand, with Simon Peter leading, said, "Lord, to whom shall we go? You have the words of eternal life'" (John 6:68). Notice again that word "eternal."

We are faced with the same choice: We are in the same situation as are the people who looked for Jesus on the other side of the lake.

What will we choose? Will we be among those who left or among those who stayed? Will we continue to ask for bread, ordinary bread, or will we instead finally forget that bread for a little while and rush forward with our hands, eyes, and souls, reaching out to receive that other bread, as we do in the Eucharist when we go to receive the Body of Christ? Those who went away saying, "This is a hard saying; who can listen to it?" were foolish. Even if they were looking for ordinary bread, if they had truly been hungry why didn't they understand that in choosing Jesus himself they would have chosen the one who had demonstrated that he knew how to multiply even ordinary bread?

We are faced with a choice at the crossroads of two paths: one for the true believers in God and one for his mere "clients." (The *clientes*, or "clients," in ancient Rome were those who crowded together every morning before the gate of the house of a rich benefactor to obtain support but cared nothing about him.) This second path is basically the one taken by the pagans: "The Gentiles," Jesus said, "seek all these things" (Matthew 6:32a)

I believe we are facing the paramount decision, the one that determines our success or failure in God's eyes. But I trust that at the very moment when I articulated the alternatives, you already made the right choice in your hearts, moved by the Holy Spirit. Like Peter, you have said,

> Lord, where can we go? We want you more than anything else. We want the living water and not the water from man-made wells; we want the living bread and not just the bread that perishes. We want healing for our souls even

more than for our bodies. We want you to remove the true, overwhelming, painful, and dreadful burden that weighs us down—our self-centeredness. We want you to heal us from that terrible tumor that we all carry within us and that leads to eternal death: sin!

"Blessed Are the Eyes Which See What You See"

Having made this fundamental choice, we can go on to ask the question that springs immediately to our lips and bring it to Jesus in the form of a humble objection. Dear Jesus, everything that you have said is fine, but allow us to ask you: How can you say that your yoke is easy and your burden light? Don't you know how terrible the suffering can be for us, and how crushing the cross is sometimes, to the point where we say, "That's it! I can't do this anymore!"—you who were moved almost to tears for the suffering of the widow of Nain as she accompanied her son for burial? Don't you know what it means to accept the yoke of the Father's will at times and to obey—you, who sweated blood in the Garden of Olives when you accepted it?

If the yoke you speak of is the law, the new law of the gospel, is it perhaps lighter or less costly than the old law of the scribes and teachers that consisted of a thousand proscriptions? Oh! Yes, it is simpler, easier to remember; it can basically be reduced to two single commands, and even to one: Love—love God and love your neighbor. But it certainly is not lighter in practice! You yourself said, shortly before your words about a light yoke, "You have heard that it was said... But I say to you...,"[21] and each time the requirement was greatly increased, and you made the yoke heavier. You said that it is not enough not to commit adultery but that we cannot even look at a man or a woman with lust in our hearts. It is not enough to love our neighbor and hate our enemies. We must also love our enemies, and not only love them with lip service. We must pray for them, do them good, and forgive them. And it is not enough to love those who love us, to greet those who greet us, and to invite those who invite us, because even the pagans do these things (see Matthew 5:17–48).

So then, what do you mean when you said that your yoke is gentle and your burden light? There is some kind of mystery here. There must be something else that we do not know about that, that would explain this paradox. There must be a hidden meaning in what Jesus is telling us.

In fact, there is, and it is called the kingdom! The thing that turns everything upside down is that with Jesus the kingdom of God has arrived. The new thing that changes everything, that explodes, so to speak, all parameters and standards of measurement, it has come. In the Gospel of Luke, soon after the section that tells of the joy that led Jesus to thank the Father for having hidden things from the wise and revealed them to infants, Jesus does not say, "Come to me, all who are weary and are carrying heavy burdens." Instead we read another of Jesus' sayings, one that has a connection to a saying in Matthew: "Then turning to the disciples he said privately, 'Blessed are the eyes which see what you see! For I tell you that many prophets and kings desired to see what you see, and did not see it, and to hear what you hear, and did not hear it'" (Luke 10:23–24).

Here is what makes the difference, the "hidden meaning"! I always remember the effect that these words from the Gospel had at the beginning of my acquaintance with the charismatic renewal. One young woman who was present at the famous retreat when the Catholic charismatic renewal was born recalled these words of Jesus and applied them to what her eyes had seen. Her words puzzled me. "What thing had this young woman seen," I asked myself, "that would make her say with such confidence, 'Blessed are the eyes which have seen what you have seen'"? I repeat these same words to you now: "Blessed are the eyes which see what you see!"

The explanation, then, is the kingdom. Things are no longer as they once were, because the standard of measurement and the "weights" have changed. The reason that the weary and oppressed find rest with Jesus and that his yoke is called easy is the same reason that the poor in the Beatitudes—those who mourn and hunger—are called "blessed." The reason is that "theirs is the kingdom of heaven" (Matthew 5:3). Can he who has the kingdom still be poor? Can he who expects a kingdom still mourn? Is having a kingdom a heavy and bitter burden?

Longing for Eternity

We can be content with the answer given to us by the word of God: the kingdom. That should be enough for us. But what will we say to the others, to those for whom the word *kingdom* means nothing? "Kingdom" is not a popular word today, in an era of republics and democracies. How will we make ourselves understood and "make a defense to any one who calls [us] to account for the hope that is in [us]" (1 Peter 3:15)?

There is, in fact, an alternative; there is another word that Scripture gives us. In fact it has often been repeated to us and we have heard it many times: "Eternity! Eternity! Eternal life!" That is the kingdom of God. That is the new standard of measurement that appeared with Jesus. It did not exist before, or it had been overlooked.

Do we want to discover the real reason that the yoke of Christ is called gentle and his yoke light? Then let us listen to the apostle Paul:

> For this slight momentary affliction [notice the words "slight" and "momentary"] is preparing for us an eternal weight of glory beyond all comparison [notice the words "eternal" and "beyond all comparison"], because we look not to the things that are seen but to the things that are unseen; for the things that are seen are transient, but the things that are unseen are eternal. (2 Corinthians 4:17–18)

A new standard of measurement has been introduced that makes crosses and trials seem slight and momentary: eternity. For that reason the same apostle can say, "I consider that the sufferings of this present time are not worth comparing with the glory that is to be revealed to us" (Romans 8:18). In contrast, everything appears slight and momentary, even tribulations, because they prepare us for that glory beyond compare.

We need to understand who the man was who called tribulation "slight" and "momentary," so that we do not make a mistake and perhaps say to ourselves, "It is easy for you, Paul, to talk like this, because you have not experienced what I have experienced and what I

SOBER INTOXICATION OF THE SPIRIT PART TWO

am going through now! I would like to see you in my shoes!" Well, the man who speaks this way is a man who, in the very same letter where he speaks about slight and momentary affliction, tells the following about himself:

> [I was] often near death. Five times I have received at the hands of the Jews the forty lashes less one [flagellation]. Three times I have been beaten with rods; once I was stoned. Three times I have been shipwrecked; a night and a day I have been adrift at sea; on frequent journeys, in danger from rivers, danger from robbers, danger from my own people, danger from Gentiles, danger in the city, danger in the wilderness, danger at sea, danger from false brethren; in toil and hardship, through many a sleepless night, in hunger and thirst, often without food, in cold and exposure. (2 Corinthians 11:23–27)

Paul's words earlier, in 2 Corinthians 4, remind us of that famous Chapter of the Mats in the history of the Franciscan movement. (The assembly was called the Chapter of the Mats because the friars were camped in huts made out of twigs and reeds.) St. Francis of Assisi, on the day of Pentecost, had gathered at St. Mary of the Angels near Assisi all the five thousand friars from around the world. At a certain point, according to *The Little Flowers*, Francis stood up and with fervor of spirit presented an ardent exhortation to those present:

> My little sons, we have promised great things [to God], but far greater things have been promised to us by God. Let us

keep those promises which we have made, and let us aspire with confidence to those things that have been promised to us. Brief is the world's pleasure, but the punishment that follows it lasts forever. Small is the suffering of this life, but the glory of the next life is infinite.[22]

We are told that after hearing the saint's speech, all the friars joyfully burst into praise and worship.

St. Francis found himself one day in San Leo, a city where a knighting festival was taking place. He climbed up a low wall and loudly proclaimed these words: "So great is the good which I expect that all pain is to me a delight."[23]

Now we have come to the heart of the issue—the word "eternity." Let us gather around this word to revive it, to warm it with our breath so that it can come back to life, because *eternity* is a dead word. We have let it die like an abandoned baby.

What has happened to this word? It was once the secret engine that stirred the Christian people to action, the North Pole that attracted their thoughts, the needle of the compass that pointed in the right direction, as it did for sailors. It was the truth that raised their hearts on high, like the gravity of the moon that raises the waters at high tide. This light has been quietly put under a bushel; the flag has been lowered as though by an army in retreat. This phenomenon has a specific name: secularization. *Secularization* means forgetting eternity, or putting it in parentheses, so that we can devote ourselves to the *seculum* (the world) and to the present time. This is considered the greatest and the most dangerous heresy of our age and, unfortunately, all of us are more or less infected by it. We are all, in that sense, heretics!

First, Marxist suspicion fell on the word *eternity*, which was said to hold people back from making a commitment to transform and improve the world and that it led to an avoidance of reality. Little by little, because of that suspicion, the word fell into oblivion and silence. Materialism and unrestrained consumerism did the rest, making it seem strange and almost in bad taste for "modern" people in step with the times to speak about eternity. Who now ever speaks about the "four last things"—death, judgment, hell, heaven—which are both the beginning and the ultimate forms of eternity?

That no one speaks about these things anymore does not mean that these realities have ceased to exist. We know how the tragedy of the ocean liner *Titanic* happened. Messages were sent by radio to signal the presence of an iceberg on the ship's route. But there was a dance on deck, so no one received the messages or took them seriously until, later that night, a terrible collision tore the boat apart and people sank into the sea. This is a picture of what can happen on a spiritual level to people who live without thinking about what might await them on their route. There is also an iceberg on our route, and it is death.

When was the last time you heard a sermon on eternal life? And yet it could be said that Jesus in the Gospels speaks about nothing else.

The very thing that Jesus in the Gospels told us to guard against has happened: "If salt has lost its taste, how shall its saltiness be restored?" (Matthew 5:13a). If believers lose their sense of eternity, who will restore it to them? The "salt of the earth" and the "light of the world" are eternity. Without them, everything loses its savor and becomes tasteless and empty, because, as St. Augustine asked, "What good is it to have a comfortable life if we cannot live forever?"[24] Earlier Jesus had asked, "What does it profit a man, to gain the whole world and forfeit his life?" (Mark 8:36).

What happens to the person who needs to weigh things when he or she has lost the scale or the standard of measurement by which everything is weighed? Picture a man holding a balance in his hand. Have you seen those balances that can be held in one hand? A flat dish on one side is held by small chains. A calibrated bar measures the weight on the other side. (This example was suggested to me by Kierkegaard's comment on Matthew 11:30.)[25] On the side with the flat plate, we put the things that are going to be weighed—wheat, bread, fish, even silver, gold, or whatever else you want—while on the other side is a graduated weight used to register the weight of the objects on the other side. If the graduated weight falls to the ground or slips, the object in the dish raises the bar higher and tips the scale toward itself. Everything being weighed, then, has the upper hand; everything—even a handful of feathers—has an easy victory, no matter how light.

This is what we have been reduced to. We have forgotten the measure of all things, which is eternity, and so earthly things have gotten the upper hand and inevitably make the balance tip in their direction. Everything seems too difficult for us, too heavy. Jesus said that if your hand causes you to sin, cut it off; if your eye causes you to sin and is an obstacle to you, pluck it out! It is better to enter into eternal life with only one hand and only one eye than with both hands and both eyes to be thrown forever into Gehenna, where the torment never stops (see Matthew 5:29–30).

Here we can see how the standard of eternity works, when it is present and operating, and what it is capable of inspiring. But for us who have lost sight of eternity, it seems extreme if we are asked to avert our eyes for an instant or to turn off the television to avoid defiling our hearts and compromising eternal life. Everything seems excessive to us: having to wake up a little earlier or to travel some distance to go to Mass, making a sacrifice for a neighbor, forgiving an offense, resisting a temptation. We immediately say to ourselves, "I cannot possibly bring myself to do this!" A woman discovers she has an unwanted pregnancy. She speaks to her husband about it. The thing seems impossible to accept, and so they choose the easiest path—abortion—which, however, can jeopardize their eternal life.

On this issue of weights and measures, let us remember the words of St. Paul: "This slight momentary affliction is preparing for us an eternal weight of glory beyond all comparison." It is slight because it is momentary; it is beyond all comparison because it is eternal! If this "weight" beyond all comparison is removed, then our affliction suddenly goes from seeming slight to seeming unbearable.

On the other hand, when you are overwhelmed by affliction on earth, throw the weight beyond all comparison—the thought of eternity—on the other side of the balance, along with your faith, and you will see that your affliction will become somewhat lighter by comparison. Let us say to ourselves, "What does this matter in the light of all eternity?" A thousand years are like a single day, like a watch in the night, like yesterday when it has passed. But what do I mean by "a single day"? It is a mere moment, a breath. Where are those years that we have lived, now that we have lived them?

I see a scenario in my mind's eye: a great crowd of diverse people who are all busy. There are those who work, those who laugh, those who cry, those who go, those who come, and those who stand off to the side, completely discouraged. Then someone arrives from far away, out of breath, an old man who whispers something to the first person he meets, and then he says it to another, always running excitedly. The one who hears it runs to repeat it to another, and these tell it to yet more people. And suddenly there is an unexpected change. Someone who was lying on the ground, discouraged, stands up and hurries to tell his relatives at home; someone who was running stops and turns back; others who were quarreling, threatening each other with clenched fists, throw their arms around each other, weeping.

What word could have produced such a change? The word *eternity*! Please forgive my boldness, but I am that old man come from afar, and all of you—or even better, all of us—we are that crowd. And the word that should be spreading among us, like a flaming torch or a signal light that watchmen used to carry from one tower to another, is still the same: Eternity! Eternity! It is eternity! They said to the Israelites exiled in Babylon, "Sing us one of the songs of Zion" (Psalm 137:3). But what did the Israelites answer their captors?

Let my tongue cleave to the roof of my mouth,
  if I do not remember you,

79

> if I do not set Jerusalem
>
> above my highest joy! (Psalm 137:6)

Let us also say, "Let my tongue cleave to the roof of my mouth if I do not remember you, heavenly Jerusalem, if I do not set Jerusalem and eternal life above all my other thoughts!"

Everyone should carry this torch home, to groups, to school, and to the workplace and light other torches with it. If someone asks you about it, then simply answer, "I found out about eternity!" And let your demeanor, by itself, indicate that this is not a joke, that it is not a slogan, and it will cause longing for eternity to spring up in whoever listens to you.

I say "longing" because I think that there is not a man or woman who does not recall a moment or a circumstance during their youthful years in which there was a feeling of eternity. It as though you stood at the door and you glimpsed it, even if you could not express any of that experience in words.

I remember a moment like that when I was in high school. It was summer, and I was hot after playing. I stretched out for a moment on the grass. My gaze was attracted to the blue sky that had light, fluffy clouds here and there. I thought, "What is beyond this blue vault, and beyond that, and even beyond that?" In successive waves, my mind rose up toward the infinite and lost itself, like someone who stares fixedly at the sun and then is blinded and cannot see anymore. The infinite recalled eternity: I went from space to time. "What does eternity mean?" I asked myself. "Always and forever! A thousand years are only the beginning; a million and a billion years are only the beginning!" Again, my mind lost itself. It was a wonderful sensation, and it made me grow.

Try sometime the experience I had. Stop, lie down on the green grass during a moment of solitude, and look at the sky. Imagine "limitless stretches / ...[and] silences more than human," as the poet Giacomo Leopardi says in his poem "The Infinite," and have the happy experience of submerging your mind in them. Submerge your mind in the sea of infinity and eternity and you too will say, as he did,

> ... in the midst
> of this immensity my thought drowns:
> and sinking is sweet to me in such a sea.[26]

Do not seek the thrill of eternity, the submersion of your mind, elsewhere, in drugs, where there is only death, illusion, and deceit. I have suggested for you a powerful antidote against the dreadful and devastating temptation of drugs. This is a way to experience a genuine feeling about eternity: Look for it above and not below, above your-selves and not down here. God will help you make it a habit. I also have some advice for older people! Stop counting your money and start counting the stars!

What happens to man if eternity is removed from his heart and his thoughts? He becomes denatured. According to the philosophers, man is a finite being with a capacity for infinity. He is open to the infinite, he needs the infinite, and he is destined for it. "You have made us for yourself," said St. Augustine, "and our heart is restless until it rests in you."[27] This is the root of the profound dissatisfaction that has taken hold of the hearts of men and women, and especially of young people. We have been made for something far different, and yet we continue to throw ourselves into the things of this world here below. Leopardi, in his poem on infinity, speaks of a "hedge, which cuts off from view / the far horizon on almost every side."[28] There is also in life, and not just in poetry, a tremendous *hedge* or barrier that prevents us from seeing beyond, the hedge of "visible things." That is why the apostle exhorted us not to fix our gaze on it.

When the world challenges you or tries to seduce you—I am speaking to everyone, but especially to the youth—by flaunting the luster of its false pearls before your eyes, its triumphant temporality, and its various kinds of intoxication (alcohol, drugs, sex, success), call on your faith and repeat to yourselves, because it is true, "Visible things last only for a moment. I am not satisfied with momentary things because I want eternal things. I want God!"

Fearlessly say to the world, You don't enchant me. You don't have a standard; you don't know eternity. It as though you are extolling the terrible power of gunpowder to someone who already knows that the atomic bomb has been invented; it is as though you are exalting the power of a short candle to bring light and warmth to someone who already has electric lights or who finds himself under a noonday sun. You lack the true standard for comparison. I have a great advantage over you. I know your power. (In fact, I know it only too well since I am also clothed in flesh and exposed to the lusts of the flesh.) You, on the other hand, don't know my power. I know what operates in you, but you don't know what operates in me and that it is stronger (see 1 John 4:4). You are actually the naïve one, not me, the believer!

The Pledge of the Holy Spirit

I know what often prevents us from speaking like this, the doubt that removes boldness from believers. The weight of eternity, it is said, will be as great as we could wish for and greater than the weight of affliction; however, we carry our crosses in time, not in eternity; our strength is temporal, not eternal. "We walk by faith, not by sight" (2 Corinthians 5:7): We have nothing, basically, to oppose to the attraction of visible things except the hope of invisible things. We have nothing to oppose to the instant gratification of things below except the promise of eternal happiness. Since the time of Augustine, people have been saying, "We want to enjoy things in this life," and, "Life is sweet."

But this is the error that believers must expose. It is not true that eternity is only a "promise" and only "an expectation" here on earth. "I write this to you who believe in the name of the Son of God," says the apostle John, "that you may know that you have eternal life" (1 John 5:13). This is one of the most vital certainties that the charismatic renewal is reviving in the Church, one of its most valuable contributions to the renewal of Christian life.

If you speak to people about eternity or eternal life, they might—if they are not believers or are nonpracticing believers—shrug and say, "Eternity, eternity! What is eternity? Who knows if this eternity of yours even exists!" What would you answer? Answer them with the words of St. John the apostle, the great cantor of eternal life:

That which was from the beginning, which we have heard, which we have seen with our eyes, which we have looked upon and touched with our hands, concerning the word of life—the life was made manifest, and we saw it, and testify to it, and proclaim to you the eternal life which was with the Father and was made manifest to us. (1 John 1:1–2)

Eternal life has indeed been made visible, because eternal life is God himself and God, in Jesus Christ, became flesh and came to dwell among us (see John 1:14). Through Jesus, eternity entered into time, and time became "weighted" with eternity. To say that Jesus is "man and God in one person" means that in him eternity and time have become united forever, in a way that is "without confusion…without division,"[29] each nature retaining its proper characteristics but in an indivisible, eternal unity.

We, too, can say about eternal life that it has been made visible to us and that we have seen it and touched it with our hands, because Jesus is alive among us. He is alive and present wherever his word is preached. He lives in his sacraments. The sacraments, in fact, and especially the Eucharist, are like windows through which eternal life bursts into our world. The saints, too, in their own way, are windows that open onto God's world, through which we are allowed to glimpse what awaits us.

Since we can have an experience of eternity through faith, from now on we can also experience happiness. Christians, like everyone else, want to be happy "while we live in this flesh," but we have discovered that there is another way to be happy. We have known the joy that is a "fruit of the Spirit" and endures affliction, the joy that is not even here on earth a "momentary" joy but a profound and lasting peace. Paul could say, "with all our affliction, I am overjoyed" (see 2 Corinthians 7:4b), and we read about the first disciples that they "were filled with joy and with the Holy Spirit" (see Acts 13:52).

Jesus' words—"Come to me all who labor and are heavy laden"—are marked by a seal, the Holy Spirit. The presence of eternal life in the Church and in each of us has a proper name: the Holy Spirit who has been given to us. He is called "the first fruits" (see Romans 8:23) and "the guarantee of our inheritance" (see Ephesians 1:14; 2 Corinthians 5:5). He has been given so that, having tasted the first fruits, we will be eager for the fullness. Because of him, we groan inwardly, waiting to enter into the freedom of the glory of the sons of God (see Romans 8:21–23). Only he can stir up in us a longing for the eternal.

We need to recognize that sometimes we seem to have forgotten about this somewhat. We behave sometimes as though the Holy Spirit were given to help us live better or as long as possible here on earth and to empower our natural lives and increase our joy of living. But the Spirit comes from on high and prods us toward heaven. He is the *ruah Yahweh*, the "breath of God" who lifts us up.

There is a new invention to make objects at the bottom of the sea float up to the surface. It fills a wrecked ship with air and detaches it from the ocean floor, and little by little the air propels the ship, which has been made lighter than water, up. Forgive me for this very earthy metaphor, but today's men and women, including Christians, are like those bodies at the bottom of the sea. We are sunk in temporality and worldliness. We have become secularized.

The Holy Spirit has been sent and has breathed into us, and he is now again being poured out in the Church for a similar purpose: to lift us up from the depths to the heights, higher and higher, so that we might turn around and contemplate the infinite sky and joyfully exclaim, "Eternity! Eternity!"

CHAPTER FIVE

The Witness to Jesus and the Spirit of Prophecy

But when the Counselor comes, whom I shall send to you from the Father, even the Spirit of truth, who proceeds from the Father, he will bear witness to me; and you also are witnesses, because you have been with me from the beginning. (John 15:26–27)

After Pentecost we see in the Church the perfect fulfillment of what Jesus said here. Peter ends his speech before the Sanhedrin: "We are witnesses to these things, and so is the Holy Spirit whom God has given to those who obey him" (Acts 5:32). This does not actually mean two distinct, independent witnesses but refers to one single witness. It means that the Paraclete "will bear witness to me through you." The Holy Spirit is the inner, invisible witness, whereas the apostles—and after them the bishops and in a different way all the disciples—are the external, visible witnesses. They lend their voices to the Spirit.

Let us reflect on this task that is still ours today: What kind of witness does Jesus expect from us? A verse from the book of Revelation seems to answer this question directly: "For the testimony of Jesus is the spirit of prophecy" (19:10). One scholar explains this brief verse this way: "The possession of the prophetic Spirit, which makes a true prophet, shows itself in a life of witness to Jesus…; all true prophets are witnesses of Jesus, and all who have the witness of Jesus in the highest sense are prophets."[30]

What Is Prophecy?

What is prophecy? An initial answer, which is somewhat sketchy but suggestive, is contained in the formula with which Balaam introduces his oracles in the book of Numbers:

The oracle of Balaam the son of Beor,
the oracle of the man whose eye is opened,
the oracle of him who hears the words of God,
and knows the knowledge of the Most High,
who sees the vision of the Almighty,
falling down, but having his eyes uncovered.
(Numbers 24:15–16)

A prophet is one who has been granted an "opened" eye that allows access to the mind of God in order to understand his secret plans. Prophecy is simultaneously a mental, visual, and auditory experience. It consists in the removal of the veil of time and space from the prophet's eyes.

At the origin of prophecy we find both of the great powers that, according to the Bible, create and move the world: the Spirit and the Word, *ruach* and *dabar*. Prophets are seen at times as men and women of the Word and at other times as men and women of the Spirit. At times a word comes upon them and constitutes them as prophets, and at other times it is the "Spirit of the Lord" (Isaiah 61:1) that comes upon them. The Lord says to Isaiah, "My spirit which is upon you, and my words which I have put in your mouth, shall not depart out of your mouth...for evermore" (59:21).

What is said about biblical inspiration in general applies in a preeminent way to prophecy. The Second Letter to Timothy contains the famous declaration "All Scripture is inspired by God" (3:16). The phrase that is translated "inspired by God" or "divinely inspired" comes from a unique word in the original language, *theopneustos*, which combines two words, one that relates to God (*theos*) and one to breathing (*pneo*). This word has two fundamental meanings; one is well known, but the other is usually overlooked, although it is not less important than the first.

The more well-known meaning is the passive one, highlighted in all the modern translations: Scripture is "inspired by God." Another passage in the New Testament explains its meaning this way: "Men moved by the Holy Spirit spoke from God" (2 Peter 1:21). This represents the classical doctrine about the divine inspiration of Scripture, which we proclaim in the creed as an article of faith, when we say that the Holy Spirit "has spoken through the prophets."

We can use human images to depict the event of inspiration that is itself mysterious. With his divine finger—that is, with the living energy that is the Holy Spirit—God "touches" that hidden place where the human spirit opens up to the infinite. From that touch—as simple and instantaneous as the God who produces it—a resonating vibration spreads through all of a person's faculties (will, intelligence, imagination, heart), translating itself into concepts, images, and words.

Now we come to the other, less well-known meaning of biblical inspiration. Grammatically, the participle *theopnuestos* is active, not passive. Scripture, said St. Ambrose, is *theopneustos* not only because it is "inspired by God" but also because it is "God-breathing"—that is, God breathes through it.[31]

The Second Vatican Council constitution *Dei Verbum* follows this second line of tradition when it says that since the Scriptures "are inspired by God [passive inspiration!] and committed once and for all time to writing, they impart the Word of God Himself without change, and make the voice of the Holy Spirit resound in the words of the prophets and apostles [active inspiration!]."[32]

St. Francis of Assisi has a stupendous image to express this. He compares the words of God to sweet-smelling, crusty loaves of bread that have just come out of the oven: "Since I am the servant of all, I am obliged to serve all and to administer to them the fragrant words of my Lord."[33]

Tongues as of Fire

There is usually only one aspect of biblical inspiration that is emphasized: inerrancy, the concept that the Bible does not contain errors.

But biblical inspiration is the basis for much more than just the simple inerrancy of the word of God (which is something negative). On the positive side, inspiration is the basis for the divine efficacy and vitality of the word.

This is the principal difference between the word of God and the words of human beings. In the Gospel of Matthew, there is a saying of Jesus that has made Gospel readers in all ages tremble: "I tell you, on the day of judgment men will render account for every careless word they utter" (Matthew 12:36).

The word translated as "careless" is *argon* in the original and means "without effect" (*a*, meaning "deprived of," plus *ergos*, meaning "effect"). Some modern translations render *argon* as "baseless," which has a passive significance and in this case means a word that has no basis and is thus slander. This is an attempt to give a more reassuring sense to Jesus' warning. However, there is nothing new here if Jesus is in fact saying that every slander must be accounted for before God! Instead the connotation of *argon* is active; it refers to a word that does not establish anything, that does not produce anything and is therefore empty, "inoperative, idle."[34]

To fully appreciate this, we need merely to contrast this adjective with the one that constantly characterizes the word of God in the Bible, the adjective *energēs*, which means "efficacious," "operative"; it is always followed by an effect (*ergos*). This is the same adjective from which we derive the word "energetic." St. Paul praises the Thessalonians because they have received the divine word of his preaching "not as the word of men" but as what it truly is, "the word of

God, which is at work [*energeitai*] in you believers" (1 Thessalonians 2:13). The Letter to the Hebrews also says, "The word of God is living and active [*energēs*]" (Hebrews 4:12).

The ineffective word that people will have to account for on the Day of Judgment is not, then, each and every empty word. It is the ineffective word spoken by any person who should instead be speaking the "energetic" words of God. It is, in brief, the word of the false prophet who does not receive the word of God but leads others to believe that it is. People will need to account for every empty word *about* God! This is the meaning of Jesus' serious admonition. The people who will need to account for every ineffective word are the people of the Church, those who are called to witness to Jesus—we ourselves!

False prophets are those who do not present the word of God in its purity but water it down and dilute it with a thousand human words. At Cana in Galilee Jesus transformed water into wine. The Spirit who gives life transforms the dead letter; this is how the Fathers interpreted this event spiritually. False prophets are those who do just the opposite: They transform the pure wine of the word of God into water that intoxicates no one, into a dead letter or into "plausible words of wisdom" (1 Corinthians 2:4).

Let us see instead how a prophetic word occurs and how it is recognized. As someone is speaking, at a certain point not determined by that person, he or she senses an interference, as if a wave on a different frequency inserts itself into his or her voice. The person becomes suddenly aware of an inner stirring, of a power and a conviction that is clearly recognized as not his or hers. The word becomes clearer and incisive. The person experiences some of the "authority" that people perceived when they heard Jesus speak (see Mark 1:22).

If, for example, someone is speaking about sin, he or she feels a zeal for God and such contempt for sin that it is as if God himself had appointed him or her as his advocate to the world. It feels to that person as though, with that power, he or she could resist the whole world and "make mad the guilty and appall the free."[35] If a person speaks of God's love or of Christ's passion, his or her voice communicates something of the very *pathos* of God. The apostle Paul describes this well:

> My speech and my message were not in plausible words of wisdom, but in *demonstration of the Spirit and of power*, that your faith might not rest in the wisdom of men but in the power of God. (1 Corinthians 2:4–5, emphasis added)

> For our gospel came to you not only in word, but also *in power and in the Holy Spirit* and with full conviction. (1 Thessalonians 1:5, emphasis added)

The apostle is speaking about something that he and his listeners have experienced. In fact, when it is the Spirit who puts a word on someone's lips, the effects, even though they are of an extremely spiritual nature, are very perceptible. Those who are listening are reached in that part of their being that no other voice can reach. They are "touched," and it is not uncommon for them to feel a tremor go through their whole body. The person speaking, and his or her voice, disappears at this point to make room for another voice.

This confirms the truth of the saying by Philo of Alexandria, a Jewish author who was a contemporary of the apostles: "The prophet, even when he seems to be speaking, really holds his peace."[36] The prophet is silent because at that moment it is no longer he or she who speaks but another. A mysterious silence occurs inside that person, as when someone moves aside respectfully to let a king pass through. That person is carried along by the word that is spoken, and if human considerations try to keep the prophet back from expressing a certain thought, he or she feels

> as it were a burning fire
>   shut up in my bones,
> and I am weary with holding it in,
>   and I cannot. (Jeremiah 20:9)

The prophet then speaks that word in a loud tone. People can be stupefied and frightened before the God who says to his messenger, a poor, sinful creature, "You shall be as my mouth" (Jeremiah 15:19).

This experience does not happen with the same intensity throughout the course of a talk or sermon. There are specific instances when God highlights only a phrase, a word. Those who proclaim and those who hear feel that droplets of fire are mixed into the words of the preacher at a certain point, making them glow.

Fire is the image that least imperfectly expresses the nature of this action by the Spirit. For this reason he manifested himself at Pentecost under the form of "tongues as of fire, distributed and resting on each one of them" (Acts 2:3). We read about Elijah that he was "like a fire, /

and his word burned like a torch" (Sirach 48:1). In Jeremiah it is God himself who says, "Is not my word like fire, says the LORD, and like a hammer which breaks the rock in pieces?" (Jeremiah 23:29).

A New Type of Prophecy

In announcing the birth of the precursor John, his father Zechariah says, "And you, child, will be called the prophet of the Most High" (Luke 1:76). Jesus says of John that he is "more than a prophet" (Matthew 11:9). But how is there prophecy in John the Baptist's case? The earlier prophets proclaimed a future salvation, but the precursor is not proclaiming a future salvation. He is pointing to someone who is already present. In what sense then can he be called a prophet?

Here is the new thing. Isaiah, Jeremiah, and Ezekiel were helping people to overcome the barrier of time. John the Baptist, on the other hand, helps people to overcome the even more difficult barrier of contradictory appearances, of scandal, of the banality and lowliness in which the appointed hour is manifested.

It is easy to believe in something grandiose and divine when it is projected into an indefinite future: "in the coming days," "in the last days," in a cosmic framework with heavens that are dripping sweetness and an earth that is opening up to bring forth the Savior. It is more difficult when the time comes to say, "Look! There he is!"—and to say it about a man whom people know everything about: where he comes from, what kind of work he does, who his mother is.

When John the Baptist says, "among you stands one whom you do not know" (John 1:26), he inaugurates the new kind of prophecy, prophecy for the Church age, which does not consist in proclaiming a distant and future salvation but in revealing the hidden presence of Christ in the world.

The innovation of Christian prophecy is not in the *nature* of prophetic speech, which is the same as it was before. It is in the *content*, which is now the person of Christ. The content no longer concerns the future but the present. Balaam said,

> I see him, but not now;
>> I behold him, but not near:
> a star shall come forth out of Jacob,
>> and a scepter shall rise out of Israel. (Numbers 24:17)

John the Baptist is not contemplating him from far off but is pointing to him in the present. His proclamation—"Behold, the Lamb of God" (John 1:29)—contains the maximum prophetic concentration, a flash of light such as we see in a short circuit. It means, "Do you remember the lamb that your ancestors sacrificed in Egypt and the meek lamb led to the slaughter that did not open its mouth? Well, all of that was a foreshadowing of the person who is before you now."

The definitive eschatological turning point has occurred. Jesus himself highlights that when he speaks of John the Baptist: "Truly, I say to you, among those born of women there has risen no one greater than John the Baptist; yet he who is least in the kingdom of heaven is greater than he.... For all the prophets and the law prophesied until John" (Matthew 11:11, 13).

One thing is clear from these words: Between the mission of John the Baptist and Jesus' mission, something has happened that is so decisive that it constitutes a watershed between two eras. History's center of gravity has shifted. The most important thing no longer lies ahead in a more or less imminent future but is in "the here and now," in the kingdom that is already operative in the person of Christ. A qualitative leap has occurred between the two proclamations. The least person in the new order is greater than the greatest person in the former order.

The theme of this eschatological turning point and fulfillment is confirmed in many other contexts in the Gospel. We need only recall such sayings by Jesus as "Behold, something greater than Jonah is here…. And behold, something greater than Solomon is here" (Matthew 12:41–42), or, "But blessed are your eyes, for they see, and your ears, for they hear. Truly, I say to you, many prophets and righteous men longed to see what you see, and did not see it, and to hear what you hear, and did not hear it" (Matthew 13:16–17). All the so-called "parables of the kingdom," like the ones about the hidden treasure and the pearl of great price (see Matthew 13:44–45), express the same basic idea: With Jesus the decisive hour in history has come. Now salvation depends on a decision for him.

An identification between the subject and the object of prophecy occurs now in Jesus. The Jesus who proclaims the Good News during his earthly life—"Jesus who preaches"—is the *subject* of the prophecy. He is the definitive prophet, the prophet par excellence, "the prophet Jesus from Nazareth," as he is called in the Gospels (Matthew 21:11). The Jesus who is proclaimed by the apostles—"Jesus preached"—is the *object* of prophecy.

The solemn inauguration of the new prophecy that has Christ as its object occurs in Peter's sermon on the Day of Pentecost:

> Men of Israel, hear these words: Jesus of Nazareth, a man attested to you by God with mighty works and wonders and signs which God did through him in your midst, as you yourselves know—this Jesus, delivered up according to the definite plan and foreknowledge of God, you crucified and killed by the hands of lawless men. But God raised him up, having loosed the pangs of death…. Let all the house of Israel therefore know assuredly that God has made him both Lord and Christ, this Jesus whom you crucified. (Acts 2:22–24, 36)

Each time I read these words, I get chills. This is the culmination of prophetic speech. What is coming to pass here is what Jesus said earlier: "But when the Counselor comes, whom I shall send to you from the Father, even the Spirit of truth, who proceeds from the Father, he will bear witness to me; and you also are witnesses, because you have been with me from the beginning" (John 15:26–27). Only now is the "veil … over [our] minds" completely lifted, because as Paul tells us, it is only "when a man turns to the Lord [that] the veil is removed" (2 Corinthians 3:15–16).

When Peter says, "This is what was spoken through the prophet Joel" (Acts 2:16), there is a flash of light such as there was in John the Baptist's preaching, but this time it is enormously more powerful, because it comes after the death and the resurrection of Christ. It is as if Peter were saying that everything the patriarchs awaited, every-thing the prophets announced and everything the psalms sang about, has become reality; it is happening now. "The promise is to you and to your children" (Acts 2:39).

The Charismatic Renewal, a Prophetic Movement

We can now ask ourselves, How is the charismatic renewal related to what I have said about prophecy in general and Christian prophecy in particular? What is its significance, and what responsibility does it have? To answer these questions, let us take a quick look at the history of this charism.

According to St. Peter's sermon at Pentecost, the Church was born entirely as a prophetic reality. All the people—sons and daughters, young and old—are now prophets (see Acts 2:17–18). This broad categorization does not, however, cancel out the specific gift of prophecy, because Paul does ask, "Are all prophets?" (1 Corinthians 12:29). There are, then, at the Church's beginning certain people who are particularly gifted with this charism and who are usually called prophets (see Acts 11:27; 15:32; 21:9–10).

In this more restricted sense, prophets, along with apostles and sometimes teachers, constitute an essential function of the Church (see Acts 13:1–3; 1 Corinthians 12:29). That specific prophetic func-tion was carried out in two forms: by community prophets, consisting of prophets who permanently live in a community, and by itinerant prophets, whom we know about especially from the *Didache*.

After the middle of the second century, prophecy quickly entered into crisis, beginning with the itinerant prophets. The leading factor in the crisis was the Montanist phenomenon that began in Asia Minor. The Montanists claimed absolute autonomy for their male and female prophets, who fell into excesses that discredited this charism in the eyes of the rest of the Church (except for Tertullian, who was their fierce defender!).

This crisis in early Church prophecy did not lead to its disappearance from the Church but rather to its institutionalization—that is, to its absorption into the sphere of the hierarchy. The charism of prophecy, like that of teaching, became more often connected to an office, to the episcopate and the hierarchy. Unless it indicated the gift of some saints to predict the future, prophecy, especially following the polemic with Protestants, was reduced to the magisterium's prerogative to interpret Scripture authentically and to teach sound doctrine.

While prophecy became *institutionalized* in the ecclesial sphere, it became *secularized* in the lay sphere. In reference to certain Old Testament prophets who exercised a critical function with respect to social and religious structures of their day, the title of "prophet" began to be given to whoever broke with traditional conventions and opened new horizons for human consciousness, even if that person was an avowed atheist. Marx, Nietzsche, and others in this category came to be called "prophets." Any religious connotation of "prophet" and any reference to the Holy Spirit disappeared.

Innovation in the concept of prophecy, as with that of charisms in general, was articulated by the Second Vatican Council. With its emphasis on the Church as the people of God, the council made room for the dialectic between institution and charism and once again highlighted the prophetic character of all the Christian people. According to one council text, Christ fulfills his prophetic office in the Church "not only through the hierarchy who teach in his name and by his power, but also through the laity. He accordingly...establishes them as witnesses."[37]

The charismatic renewal, together with other postconciliar developments, represents the actualization of this rediscovery in the life of the Church. It is first of all a prophetic movement before it is a charismatic movement. The charismatic renewal is the rediscovery and proclamation of the lordship of Christ that, as we have seen, represents the quintessence of Christian prophecy. Even after thirty years I remember the emotion I felt on hearing forty thousand people singing one evening at the 1977 Kansas City Conference of the Charismatic Renewal.

> He is Lord, He is Lord.
> He is risen from the dead, and He is Lord.
> Every knee shall bow, every tongue confess,
> that Jesus Christ is Lord.

On Good Friday of 2008, in St. Peter's Basilica and in the presence of the Holy Father, speaking about the unity of all Christians, I recalled an event from that meeting in Kansas City. One night a presenter began to speak into the microphone in a way that at that time was strange to me: "You priests and pastors, mourn and weep, because the body of my son is broken.... You laymen and laywomen, mourn and weep, because the body of my son is broken."

I began to see people, one after another, fall to their knees around me, many of them sobbing in repentance for the divisions in the body of Christ. A banner that read "Jesus is Lord" stretched from one end of the stadium to the other. I was there as an observer who was still somewhat critical and detached, but I remember thinking to myself, "This is a prophecy for the Church. If all believers were someday to unite as one church, it would look like this: We would be on our knees with humble and contrite hearts, under the great lordship of Christ."

Paul VI, when greeting members of the charismatic renewal in 1975, said that his motto could have been a phrase from the hymn of St. Ambrose: "*Laeti bibamus sobriam profusionem Spiritus,*" Let us drink the sober intoxication of the Spirit with joy.[38] However, I have always thought that an even more pertinent motto is the verse, from Psalms, that someone used at the beginning of the renewal: "*Reddite Deo potentiam suam*" (Psalm 68:34), Give back the power to God.[39]

There is a specific contribution of the renewal to the rediscovery of the prophetic dimension of the Church; it consists in bringing back the importance that prophecy had in the early Christian community as well as the expressions of that prophecy. We only need to reread 1 Corinthians 14 to realize how similar people's experience in the renewal in its best moments has been to that of the early Christians:

> Earnestly desire the spiritual gifts, especially that you may prophesy.... He who prophesies speaks to men for their upbuilding and encouragement and consolation.... Now I want you all to speak in tongues, but even more to prophesy.... If...the whole Church assembles and all speak in tongues,

and outsiders or unbelievers enter, will they not say that you are mad? But if all prophesy, and an unbeliever or outsider enters, he is convicted by all, he is called to account by all, the secrets of his heart are disclosed; and so, falling on his face, he will worship God and declare that God is really among you. (1 Corinthians 14:1, 3, 5, 23–25)

How many times what Paul says has been repeated in meetings of our own time! Nonbelievers and skeptics, accidentally ending up at one of these meetings or perhaps urged by someone to come, have found themselves exclaiming, "God is here!" This happened to me, too.

It was 1975, and I was invited to a prayer group in Rome. I came with quite a critical attitude, so the leader was telling people, "Do not go to that friar. He is an enemy of the renewal!" However, seeing a priest among them, some of them asked me to hear their confessions. It was the first real charismatic shock of my life. I had never seen such genuine repentance. Sins seemed to fall away from their souls like stones, and there were tears of joy at the end. I could only say to myself, "God is here!"

But as Origen told us, "*Ipsa novitas innovanda est*" (Newness itself must be renewed).[40] Even the renewal needs to be renewed. What remains of the strong prophetic character of the early days? The apostle's exhortation to Timothy is also addressed to us: "I remind you to rekindle the gift of God that is within you through the laying on of my hands" (2 Timothy 1:6). "To rekindle" (*anazopurein*) literally means "to blow on the flame," "to remove the ashes in order to revive the fire again." Let us not hand on a dim flame and a smoldering wick to the new generations that are starting to learn about the reality of the renewal.

Prerequisites for Prophecy: Humility and Love

At this point I need to say something about the "human element" in prophecy, the dispositions of a soul that encourage its exercise. In other words, what should we do so that the prophetic charism is "rekindled" in us?

The first requirement is *prayer*. We have heard what Jesus said to his apostles: "And you also are witnesses, because you have been with me from the beginning" (John 15:27). We need first of all to be "with Jesus," listening to him and contemplating his face to discern what he is saying and to understand his plans. Without prayer, no prophecy! However, I will not stress this theme, because it is obvious.

I need to point out two other requirements that are equally vital: *humility* and *love*. The prophet, as we heard from Philo, "even when he seems to be speaking, really holds his peace"; he or she recedes to make room for another voice. Seeking after one's own glory extinguishes prophecy, just as sand and dirt thrown on top of flames put out the fire. On the other hand, a renunciation of one's own glory gives free rein to the Spirit.

We have the most obvious example of this in the apostles themselves. We all know that in emphasizing the phenomenon of tongues, the author of Acts wanted to establish a parallel and an antithesis with Babel. At Babel everyone spoke the same language, but at a certain point they could not understand each other. At Pentecost all spoke different languages—that is the reason for the long list of peoples in

Acts 2:9–11—but everyone understood the apostles. Why?

Let us listen to what the builders of Babel say when they prepare to begin their work: "Come, let us build ourselves a city, and a tower with its top in the heavens, and let us make a name for ourselves; otherwise we shall be scattered abroad upon the face of the whole earth" (Genesis 11:4). They wanted to build a temple to a divinity (a famous tower, a ziggurat, a temple with terraces). But they did so to make a name for themselves, for their own glory and not for God's glory. God was being used, so the confusion of languages was a result.

Now let us come to Pentecost. All the people understand the apostles as they proclaim "God's deeds of power" (Acts 2:11). Before the coming of the Spirit, the apostles also wanted to make a name for themselves, discussing among themselves who was the greatest (see Mark 9:34). This is no longer the case. They have forgotten about themselves and are completely taken with and amazed by God's glory. This attitude confers an irresistible prophetic power to their proclamation: "You crucified and killed [Jesus].... But God raised him up.... Repent...and you will receive the gift of the Holy Spirit" (Acts 2:23, 38). This outlines the path to prophecy: Remove the focus from ourselves and refocus on Christ.

The other requirement, as I said earlier, is *love*. God is love and speaks through love. Love is the frequency on which he transmits his word. It is love, above all, for the people to whom he was sent.

Remember the story of Jonah. There is a message there that often eludes us. Why does Jonah look for a way to avoid going to Nineveh to preach? Because he does not love the Ninevites; they are Israel's enemies. When he is finally forced to go to Nineveh, he begins to preach, "Yet forty days, and Nin'eveh shall be overthrown!" (Jonah 3:4). And we see that the prospect of its destruction is not in the least displeasing to him.

But what happens after that? God is moved and forgives the Ninevites. Jonah becomes angry, and God needs to explain to him patiently why he could not destroy all of those poor people who are so ignorant that they cannot tell their right hand from their left. (Sometimes God works harder at converting the preacher than at converting all the people to whom he is sent!) Jonah lacks love. When there is no love, the words we preach become like rocks, and people shield themselves from rocks.

God says to Moses, "I have seen the affliction of my people who are in Egypt; and have heard their cry. . . . I know their sufferings" (Exodus 3:7). Christ is moved when he sees the crowd; he sees that they are "harassed and helpless, like sheep without a shepherd" (Matthew 9:36). The prophet is someone who shares the *pathos* of God and the compassion of Christ. If we do not have these sentiments, there is only one thing to do: Ask the Holy Spirit to put them in our hearts and to let us participate to some extent in the love of Christ for all the people he has redeemed by his blood. "For the love of Christ controls us, because we are convinced that one has died for all" (2 Corinthians 5:14).

We Are All Prophets!

The New Testament, as I said, speaks of two types of prophets: prophets in a general sense and those who have a prophetic charism recognized by their community. Not everyone is the second kind of prophet, but everyone is the first kind. We know the prophecy of Joel that Peter saw fulfilled at Pentecost:

> And in the last days it shall be, God declares,
> that I will pour out my Spirit upon all flesh,
> and your sons and your daughters shall prophesy,
> and your young men shall see visions,
> and your old men shall dream dreams;
> yes, and on my menservants and my maidservants in those
>   days
> I will pour out my Spirit; and they shall prophesy.
> (Acts 2:17–18)

The Second Vatican Council has reaffirmed the prophetic vocation of all the people of God: "All the members [of the Church] ought to reverence Jesus in their hearts...and by the spirit of prophecy give testimony to Jesus."[41] This is precisely the innovation created by Christ's coming and the pouring out of his Spirit. In the Old Testament only some people, and only in particular circumstances, were prophets. Today every Christian shares that vocation.

The prospect of being prophets should not frighten us. We are not prophets only through speaking—or, better, we are prophets who speak, but we speak not only with our mouths but also with our eyes, our hands, our lives. Paul VI said, "The Church needs a perennial Pentecost; she needs fire in her heart, the word on her lips, a look that is prophetic."[42]

A look that is prophetic! At the beginning of the renewal, a priest was going home on the train after a charismatic retreat. Charismatic songs were still echoing within him. At a certain point a distinguished lady who was facing him folded the newspaper she was reading, looked at him, and said, "Do you know what, Father? You have a face that makes a person believe in God." How I wish that people could say or think the same thing when they meet any Catholic!

John the Baptist teaches us that to be prophets, in the Christian sense of the word, we do not need great erudition and eloquence. He is not a great theologian; his Christology is poor and rudimentary. He does not yet know the loftiest titles for Jesus: Son of God, the Word, Son of Man, and so on. Nevertheless, how well he succeeds in making people understand the grandeur and uniqueness of Christ! He uses the simplest images of a peasant: "I am not worthy to untie the thong of his sandals" (see John 1:27). The world and all of humanity, according to John's words, seem to be contained in a sieve that this Messiah holds in his hands. Before him it is determined who stands and who falls, who is good wheat and who is chaff that the wind will scatter.

However, be careful not to cut the content of Christian prophecy in half. It is true that it essentially consists in the proclamation of the lordship of Christ, but he himself taught us that this lordship is inseparable from concern for the poor and their suffering: "The Spirit of the Lord is upon me, because he has anointed me to bring good news to the poor" (Luke 4:18). That good news is that

Blessed are you poor, for yours is the kingdom of God.

...

But woe to you that are rich, for you have received your consolation. (Luke 6:20, 24)

We cannot proclaim, "Jesus is Lord," and then say, "Get away from us, you foreigners." We cannot remain indifferent before the spectacle of a few successful people (who are often only clever and unscrupulous), who have everything and parade it in front of others, while hundreds of thousands of families have nothing to feed their children and stand at the cash register at the supermarket with only one tomato because that is all they can afford.

After the prophet Isaiah was purified by the burning coal and realized he was a man of unclean lips, he heard a mysterious voice saying, "Whom shall I send, and who will go for us?" Without hesitation he replied, "Here am I! Send me" (Isaiah 6:8). This call is still taking place. Let us also cry out—but only if we are serious in saying it—"Here am I, Lord. Send me!"

CHAPTER SIX

Born of Water and the Spirit

Rebirth From Above and the Baptism of the Spirit

The theme of this chapter comes from John 3:5: "Truly, truly, I say to you, unless one is born of water and the Spirit, he cannot enter the kingdom of God." It is characteristic of Johannine theology to define Christian life as a "new birth," a "birth from above" (see John 3:3), or as a "birth from God," just as it is characteristic of Pauline theology to define it as a "new creation." At times, rebirth is attributed to faith: "to all who received him who *believed* in his name, he gave power to become children of God" (John 1:12, *emphasis added*). At times, as in the John 3:5 text, it is attributed to water and the Spirit—that is, to baptism. However, all of this refers to the same event. In some instances, the role of a human being (faith) is emphasized; in other instances, God's role (the sacrament). At times the role of grace and at other times the role of freedom is emphasized.

I would like to illustrate the relationship between the birth from above that John speaks about and the baptism or outpouring of the Spirit that we see occurring in the charismatic renewal. The expression "one baptism" (Ephesians 4:5) goes back to St. Paul. The Church has inserted the statement "I believe in one baptism for the remission of sins" in its creed to oppose those (Novationists, Donatists) who proposed the necessity of being rebaptized after apostasy or after having joined heretical sects. Baptism is the new birth, and, as in the natural order, a person is born only once. What we call baptism of the Spirit cannot, then, be the new birth or an absolute beginning. It is a renewal and an actualization of baptismal birth, a conscious awareness and a powerful experience of its meaning and its potentialities.

I have given elsewhere the theological explanation of the relationship between the sacrament of baptism and what is called the "baptism of the Spirit."[43] It is based on the concept of a sacrament that is "unreleased" but that can be revived once the obstacle (*obex*) that impeded full efficacy is removed.[44] In the case of baptism, the obstacle, of course, is not sin but rather the lack of personal faith and conscious acceptance of Christ as one's Lord when one has reached adulthood.

One example that everyone can understand is a limb, a hand, or a foot that has fallen asleep. Everyone has at some time experienced this. It can happen when someone remains motionless for too long, because of a certain posture, or for other reasons. The blood circulation is stopped and one loses feeling in the limb. Something similar happens in a spiritual organism when its spiritual capabilities remain unused after baptism: The circulation of the Holy Spirit is reduced or stopped. The weakness of the Church is that it has too many hands and feet that have fallen asleep!

The baptism or outpouring of the Spirit is the special grace of the renewal. It is also our specific contribution to the Church's current effort toward a new evangelization. All the movements raised up by the Spirit after Vatican Council II are animated by an eagerness to evangelize, and each of them translates that into practice according to its proper charism. The special charism of the charismatic renewal turns out to be precisely the baptism of the Spirit. Through the Life in the Spirit Seminars that precede the baptism in the Spirit, the charismatic renewal introduces many people to a knowledge of the fundamental truths of faith and through the experience of the Spirit transforms many nominal Christians into authentic Christians.

Woe to the charismatic renewal if it neglects this grace. In many parts of the world, people bemoan a downturn in the strength of the renewal and of its ability to attract young people and change people's lives. However, one thing that everyone observes is certain: The power of the Spirit is not diminished—"The LORD's hand is not shortened" (Isaiah 59:1a)! Those who receive the baptism of the Spirit with the appropriate dispositions experience exactly the same fruits today that our ancestors did so many years ago. I would like to highlight some of these fruits specifically to make us eager to have them in our lives.

The expression "baptism of the Holy Spirit" was not invented by the charismatic renewal or by the Pentecostal movement that preceded it. As we all know, it comes from Jesus himself, who said to the apostles before he ascended into heaven, "John baptized with water, but before many days you shall be baptized with the Holy Spirit" (Acts 1:5). What people do not always pay attention to is that not only did Jesus use the words "to baptize with the Spirit" but he also indicated their significance and meaning. What happened not "many days" from then—and to be precise ten days later? Pentecost!

If the baptism of the Spirit, the way that Jesus meant it, points primarily and directly to Pentecost, then the simplest, and even necessary, way for us to understand its significance and its effects is to look at what happened at Pentecost—to see what the effects were in the lives of the apostles and of the budding Church, and to see what happens today to those who have received the baptism of the Spirit and experienced a new Pentecost.

I would like, therefore, to look at the account of Pentecost in light of the experience of the charismatic renewal and, conversely, to look at the experience of the charismatic renewal in light of the account of Pentecost. I will look at certain parts of the text and highlight what they help us understand about the baptism of the Spirit.

All Were Filled with the Holy Spirit

> When the day of Pentecost had come, they were all together in one place. And suddenly a sound came from heaven like the rush of a mighty wind, and it filled all the house where they were sitting. And there appeared to them tongues as of fire, distributed and resting on each one of them. And they were all filled with the Holy Spirit. (Acts 2:1–4a)

What does it mean that "they were all filled with the Holy Spirit"? The answer is simple. All we have to do is ask ourselves who the Holy Spirit is. He is, in the Trinity, the love that flows between the Father and the Son, a love so strong and substantial that it constitutes a "subsisting relationship," a person. To say that "they were all filled with the Holy Spirit," then, means that they were filled with the love of God and that the apostles had an overwhelming experience of being loved by God. Only this can explain the sudden and radical change that happened to them, which the rest of the text will clearly show.

Paul explains Pentecost this way: "God's love has been poured into our hearts through the Holy Spirit who has been given to us" (Romans 5:5). To say that they were filled with the love of God is like saying that they were filled with God, because "God is love" (1 John 4:8b)!

This interpretation of Pentecost is uniquely confirmed by the experience of those who have received the baptism of the Spirit. One of its clearest and most attested fruits is a new experience of God's love, and for many it is the startling and wondrous discovery of that reality. The people who attended the retreat at Duquesne University that began the charismatic renewal in the Catholic Church confess that there was a moment when they "feared being loved too much." It was as though "Yahweh on Mt. Sinai...had come into the room and filled both it and us."[45] Countless numbers of people have described the moment of their baptism of the Spirit as an experience of a "flood of love" descending on them. For some it is an immediate sensation that results in tears of joy; for others, it is an awareness that grows over time.

You may have noticed in what I just said that I often used the word "experience." We need to pause a bit here on this topic, because it allows us to become aware of one of the most notable contributions of the charismatic renewal to Christian theology and spirituality. One of the things that most impresses (and sometimes scandalizes) outside observers of the Pentecostal and charismatic phenomenon is how an inner experience of the Spirit results in the involvement of one's whole being, body and soul: the lifting and clapping of hands, closed eyes, ecstatic faces, smiles, tears—not to mention speaking or singing in tongues and other phenomena. I must confess that at the beginning I had trouble accepting all this myself.

We know that the word "enthusiasm" does not enjoy good standing among scholars of the history of Christianity, but there is more than one kind of enthusiasm. There is a good kind of enthusiasm that in the patristic tradition was called the "sober intoxication" of the Spirit. What other word could we possible use to describe the attitude of the apostles on the day of Pentecost? What do we think led some of those present to believe that the apostles were "filled with new wine" (Acts 2:13b)? "These men are not drunk, as you suppose" (Acts 2:15a), St. Peter explained, and St. Cyril of Jerusalem comments, "They are drunk, [but] not as you suppose. They are drunk with a sober drunkenness, deadly to sin, and vivifying to the heart."[46]

Pentecost is the moment when a heart of stone is shattered and a heart of flesh takes its place, but this heart "transplant" does not occur under general anesthesia! We are used to thinking of everything in abstract and conceptual terms: A human being, through baptism, becomes a child of God, a member of the body of Christ; the Holy Spirit comes to dwell in that person who then receives sanctifying grace, theological virtues, etc. However, all of this transpires on an unconscious level without any of it being "noticed" on the existential and emotional level.[47] This is precisely the missing dimension that the charismatic renewal helps the Church to deal with. This was not always and everywhere the case, especially before scholastic theology was established in the West.

The contribution of the charismatic renewal and in particular of the baptism of the Spirit in restoring this precious element of Christian tradition was recognized by the great theologian Karl Rahner, who writes concerning charismatic experiences: "Here we are certainly confronted with especially impressive, humanly affective, liberating experiences of grace which offer wholly novel existential horizons. These mould the innermost attitude of a Christian for a long time, and are quite fit...to be called 'baptism in the Spirit.'"[48]

Charisms and Holiness
Acts 2:14 begins a new section in the account of Pentecost that deals with Peter's response to the accusation of being drunk with wine:

These men are not drunk, as you suppose, since it is only the third hour of the day; but this is what was spoken by the prophet Joel:

"And in the last days it shall be, God declares,

that I will pour out my Spirit upon all flesh,

and your sons and your daughters shall prophesy,

and your young men shall see visions,

and your old men shall dream dreams;

yea, and on my menservants and maidservants in those days

I will pour out my Spirit, and they shall prophesy."

(Acts 2:15–18)

This text mentioning prophecy, visions, dreams, and miracles gives us an opportunity to touch on a fundamental point for understanding all of biblical pneumatology and to become aware of the existence of two different kinds of effects of the baptism of the Spirit.[49]

The Bible shows the Spirit acting in two different ways. The first, which we can call *charismatic*, presents the Spirit as a power that comes upon certain people at certain times and confers on them the ability to perform actions or utter words beyond their human abilities. The Spirit suddenly comes upon a person and fills him or her with wisdom; he confers artistic gifts on another person to embellish the temple (see Exodus 31:3–6; 35:31–33). He comes upon someone else and confers the gift of prophecy (see Micah 3:8) or gifts of ruling (see Isaiah 11:2–4) or supernatural strength to deliver the people (see Judges 13:25).

The second way the Spirit acts, which we can call *sanctifying*, is seen later, after the exile. Ezekiel speaks of a new Spirit that can change people's hearts and give them the ability to obey God's laws (see Ezekiel 36:26–27). In Psalm 51, the Spirit is called "holy" (v. 11) for the first time, and the purifying and renewing of one's inner being is attributed to him.

The fundamental difference between the two is that in charismatic action the Spirit enters into a person but does not stop there. The Spirit's goal is not the spiritual improvement of that person but rather the good of the community. A person might not become holier because of the charism received and can even abuse the gift and turn it into a reason for condemnation, as we see in the stories of Saul and Solomon. In contrast to this, sanctifying action remains within the people who receive the Spirit, transforming them from the inside and making them precious to God. In theology, a charism is defined as a "grace freely given" (*gratis data*), while sanctifying action is defined as "grace that makes one pleasing (to God)" (*gratum faciens*).

The distinction becomes even clearer in the New Testament. The first mode of action is clearly seen in the texts that describe charisms and the operations of the Spirit, first of all in Jesus' life and then in the life of the Church. The second kind of action is defined as the sanctifying action of the Spirit (Titus 2:4; 1 Peter 1:2) and consists in the new life in the Spirit and, concretely, in charity. In 1 Corinthians 12–14, Paul summarizes this twofold mode of the Holy Spirit's operation, speaking first about charisms and then about love. He insists on the superiority of love over charisms, but he recognizes that both are necessary for the building up of the body of Christ.

Both of these kinds of effects are produced through the baptism of the Spirit. The most common fruit in those who receive it, as we have seen, is a new experience of God's love. Christian life is lived out according to the "law of the Spirit" that leads us to do things through attraction and not constraint, through love and not fear, joyfully and spontaneously. People have a personal experience of the Holy Spirit, of his anointing in prayer, of his consolation during trials, of his guidance in their decisions. They experience joy in praising God, and their minds are opened to understand Scripture. All of these things are effects of the interior sanctifying action of the Holy Spirit.

The very name "charismatic renewal," however, also attests the importance that is ascribed to charisms. From this point of view, it seems to be God's answer to John XXIII's prayer for "a new Pentecost." At the heart of the renewal there has been, and still is, a certain tension between the two kinds of activity of the Spirit. Some emphasize the importance of personal sanctification, and thus of sacraments, prayer, and the acquisition of virtue. Others, without denying these things, place great importance on the exercise of charisms and in particular the charism of healings.

The lesson that comes to us from the Bible in its account of Pentecost and from the same teachings of Vatican Council II is that these two aspects need to be kept united; in addition, we must respect the variety of gifts and rejoice rather than be distressed if others have gifts different from ours. Nevertheless, there is a hierarchy between the two kinds of activities of the Spirit, and we need to acknowledge the priority of personal sanctification as the indispensable condition either for a healthy exercise of the charisms or for evangelization.

Particularly with regard to personal sanctification, I feel the need to offer an observation. In the renewal, people who gather together come from very different life situations. There is an increasing number of broken marriages and legal separations. How should we respond to brothers and sisters who are in these situations and are seeking the Church's help in the renewal?

First, a distinction needs to be made. If the breakup happened in the past, regardless of whether it was that person's fault, and it is not possible to go back—for example. in the case of divorced people who have remarried (and perhaps have children in the new marriage)—nothing forbids us from welcoming these people to prayer groups and praying for an outpouring of the Spirit on them. The Church has often reasserted that this situation prevents access to the Eucharist but not to the Church's prayer. Since the outpouring of the Spirit is not a sacrament but rather a prayer and a spiritual help, nothing, in my opinion, forbids people, after a good confession and sincere repentance, from being prayed over to receive the gift of the Spirit.

The situation is different if things are currently taking place, if marriages are in crisis now but not yet broken up, because once the spouses get to know the Lord, with the help of his grace and their willingness, marriages can be healed. Here, I need to give a rather severe admonition. We must not play games with God. One cannot look for approval from the renewal as a way of bypassing the requirements of conscience and of the Church.

Experience shows that the grace of the Spirit can restore dead marriages and confer on them a splendor and a vitality that was previously unknown. I know of several such cases myself. However, people need to give the Spirit the freedom to do that work. At times a person does not want the marriage restored, perhaps because his or her heart is already tied to someone else and is hardened. In this case prayer for the outpouring of the Spirit should be denied, because it could do more harm than good by giving someone the false security of being in good standing with his or her conscience and with the Church.

The Discovery of the Lordship of Christ

Let us look at a subsequent passage in the Pentecost account. We will discover another fruit of the baptism of the Spirit, perhaps the best fruit. After responding to the assumption of those who believed the apostles were drunk with wine, Peter continues his sermon with this passage that we read earlier:

> Men of Israel, hear these words: Jesus of Nazareth, a man attested to you by God with mighty works and wonders and signs which God did through him in your midst, as you yourselves know—this Jesus, delivered up according to the definite plan and foreknowledge of God, you crucified and killed by the hands of lawless men. But God raised him up, having loosed the pangs of death, because it was not possible for him to be held by it. (Acts 2:22–24)

A long quotation from Psalm 16 follows at this point to demonstrate from Scripture that the Messiah could not remain in the grave, and the sermon ends with a solemn declaration—almost a dogmatic definition "*urbi et orbi*"[50]—to Israel and to the world: "Let all the house of Israel therefore know assuredly that God has made him both Lord and Christ, this Jesus whom you crucified" (Acts 2:36).

So many teachings are contained in this very beginning of the apostolic preaching! First of all we learn this: The first effect of the coming of the Spirit is an irresistible impulse to proclaim Christ. Only now, thanks to the Spirit, are the apostles guided into "all the truth" about Jesus (see John 16:12). They understand its universal dimension now. They understand that because of what happened in him a few weeks earlier, the destiny of all of humanity is no longer the same. "Let all the house of Israel know," was the equivalent of saying, "Let all the world know." We can perceive, along with a new understanding about Christ, a new love for him. Peter is now ready to give his life for him, and indeed he will do so.

We can ask ourselves at this juncture: If this is the high point of Pentecost, how are people renewed through the baptism of the Spirit now? What new understanding about Christ is demonstrated by those who received him? The most significant thing is their rediscovery of a foundational biblical truth: Jesus Christ is Lord! The most inspired and most beloved songs of the charismatic renewal are those that proclaim the lordship of Christ: "He is Lord, he is Lord."

St. Paul speaks about a knowledge of Christ that is of "surpassing worth" (Philippians 3:8), a sublime knowledge that consists in knowing and proclaiming him as Lord. It is this proclamation, together with faith in the resurrection of Christ, that saves a human being (see Romans 10:9). And that knowledge is made possible only by the Holy Spirit: "No one can say 'Jesus is Lord' except by the Holy Spirit" (1 Corinthians 12:3b).

This rediscovery of Jesus as Lord, which is experiential and not just intellectual, is, I believe, one of the most significant theological and spiritual contributions that the baptism of the Spirit brings to the charismatic renewal and that the charismatic renewal brings to the Catholic Church. Entire books can be written on Christ as *Kyrios* [Lord] without giving any indication of being touched in the least by the lordship of Christ, like people who speak about fire without ever stretching forth their hands to feel its warmth. The difference between the Lord Jesus known through books and the Lord Jesus as revealed by the Holy Spirit is like the difference between a sky that is painted on canvas and the real sky overhead.

The new relationship with the Lord Jesus results—precisely as it did on the day of Pentecost—in the necessity of proclaiming Christ to others, in the impulse to evangelize. For me this need resulted in a decision to leave university teaching and to dedicate myself full-time to the ministry of the word of God.

Baptism of the Spirit Leads to the Church

The last section of the Pentecost account contains this well-known description of the Christian community:

> Those who received his word were baptized, and there were added that day about three thousand souls. And they held steadfastly to the apostles' teaching and fellowship, to the breaking of the bread and to the prayers.... And the Lord added to their number day by day those who were being saved. (Acts 2:41–42, 47b)

The most important teaching here is not "how" the community is presented, its daily life, but the very fact that it exists. It shows that those who received the gift of the Spirit were not left to themselves, each of them on his own, but were "added," or incorporated, into a community. The word *church* did not yet exist, but that is what this passage is describing. In the encyclical *Dominum et Vivificantem*, John Paul II affirms that "the *era of the Church* began with the 'coming,' that is to say the descent of the Holy Spirit on the apostles gathered together in the Upper Room in Jerusalem, together with Mary, the Lord's Mother."[51] Pentecost is the birthday of the church.

From this alone we learn that just as the Spirit leads to Christ, so too the Spirit leads to the church. St. Irenaeus has a famous text on this issue that is still fully relevant: "This gift of God [the Holy Spirit] has been entrusted to the Church...to this end that all the members receiving it might have life.... They do not partake who have left the Church. For where the church is, there is the Spirit if God."[52]

Because the recent experience of the baptism in the Spirit began among Pentecostal groups, there is a fear that the charismatic renewal, and in particular the baptism of the Spirit, could lead people in the opposite direction, that is, toward individualism and anti-institutionalism. This has almost always happened to charismatic and prophetic groups in the past, starting with the Montanists in the second century. It is striking that this has not happened and that the Catholic charismatic renewal was born with a strong ecclesial orientation, which the hierarchy noticed, defining it, in the words of Paul VI, as "a chance for the Church."[53]

The situation we are living in demands that we be renewed in this original ecclesial vocation. The Church is under accusation; will there also be some among us who will accuse her? Will we withdraw our loyalty to the Church because of the things we hear said about her? Let us hear Paul's words in his Letter to the Ephesians: "Christ loved the Church and gave himself up for her, that he might sanctify her, having cleansed her by the washing of the water of the word, that he might present the Church to himself in splendor, without spot or wrinkle or any such thing, that she might be holy and without blemish" (5:25b–27).

The apostle's assertion inevitably raises a question: "Christ loved the Church," but what about you? Do you love the Church? Many Christians continue to say, or at least to think, "I love Christ but not the Church." They do not realize that with this approach they deprive themselves not only of the Church but of Christ as well. You cannot have the bridegroom without the bride. St. Cyprian said, "He cannot have God as a father who does not have the Church as a mother."[54]

We know the objection: What about the disarray in the Church? And the clergy scandals? Don't we think that Jesus knows the sins of the Church better than we do? Didn't he know for whom he was dying? Didn't he know that among his disciples one had betrayed him, another was about to deny him, and all but one of them were about to run away? But he loved this Church that was real—and not another that was ideal or imaginary. He died to make the Church "holy and without blemish" and not because she was already holy and without blemish. He loved the Church "in hope" not only for what she "is" but also for what she is called to be and "will be": the heavenly Jerusalem "prepared as a bride adorned for her husband" (Revelation 21:2).

Christ loved the Church and gave himself for her so that she would be "without spot," and the Church would be without spots if we were not part of her! The Church would have one less wrinkle if I would have committed one less sin. Erasmus of Rotterdam once said the following to Martin Luther, who was reproving him for remaining in the Catholic Church in spite of her "corruption": "I put up with this church until I see a better one, and it is forced to put up with me until I become better."[55]

Should we then always remain silent? No. Once we have "come home," once we have wept with the Church and have humbled ourselves at her feet, God can command you, as he has others in the past, to lift up your voice against "the evils of the Church," but not before you are ready to die like a grain of wheat for its sake. Antonio Rosmini,[56] Fr. Primo Mazzolari,[57] and Fr. Lorenzo Milani,[58] not to mention others from more recent years, have lifted their prophetic voices against the evils in the Church, but they never withdrew their loyalty and submission to her. One of them in particular, Fr. Mazzolari, has penned words that should cause many of the Church's critics to reflect:

> Lord, I am your weak flesh. I weigh on you like a heavy cross that no shoulder can support. So as not to leave me when I am down, you also carry my burden yourself and walk as well as you can with it. Among those whose burdens you carry,

there are those who accuse you of not walking according to the rules and even accuse your Church of being slow. They forget that, although burdened as she is by human faults, your Church cannot and will not throw anyone back into the sea (they are her children!) and that carrying all her children counts for more than arriving.[59]

To those who urged him to break with the institutional Church, which opposed him, Fr. Milani answered, "We will not leave the Church because we cannot live without the sacraments and its teaching."[60]

In many European countries and in the United States, many Catholics are abandoning the Church, even officially. They are removing themselves from being listed as its members. In an analogous situation, when many were leaving him, Jesus addressed to his apostles a dramatic question that the Church now addresses to you: "Will you also go away?" (John 6:67). Like Peter, we respond with conviction. In unison, we say, "Holy Mother Church, to whom else should we go? Who else will absolve us from our sins, or give us the Body of Christ, or speak words of eternal life to us?"

This concludes my analysis of the significance of the baptism of the Spirit and its fruits. I have emphasized only a few fruits, but in practice they are much more numerous and diverse. Of course, none of them is automatic or present in everyone in the same way and at the same time. As with all of God's gifts, they must be received and cultivated with constancy and perseverance and through the discipline of the cross. This explains why, after the enthusiasm and intoxication at the outset, many lose the graces they received through the baptism of the Spirit and return to the life they had before.

As for the analysis of the cause for this, I will leave that for another time. At this point, it is fitting to recall positively the wonderful fruits that the baptism of the Spirit can bring—and has in fact brought—to millions of people. That recollection can serve to kindle in us the desire to return to experiencing these fruits with the intensity we once had and to increase our commitment so that many others in the Church may have this experience.

I am convinced that the charismatic renewal—in all its national and supranational expressions—is the apple of the eye of the Risen Lord. We must consider it a point of honor and a duty of gratitude on our part to keep it healthy.

NOTES

1. Bishop Ignatius Hazim of Latakia (later the Patriarch of Antioch as of 1979) in *The Uppsala Report 1968: Official Report of the Fourth Assembly of the World Council of Churches, Uppsala July 4–20, 1968,* Norman Goodall, ed. (Geneva: World Council of Churches, 1969), p. 298. The text has been set as poetry to highlight the ideas.

2. Augustine, *Confessions* 8.11.27, John K. Ryan, trans. (Garden City, N.Y.: Image, 1960), p. 201.

3. Augustine, *Confessions* 8.11.25–26, pp. 199–200.

4. Cf. Augustine, *Confessions* 8.12.28, p. 202: "How long, how long? Tomorrow and tomorrow? Why not now? Why not in this very hour an end to my uncleanness?"

5. See Revelation 2:2, 19; 3:1b, 8, 15.

6. Quoted in *The Spirit and the Church*, Ralph Martin, ed. (New York: Paulist, 1976), p. 16.

7. *Legend of Perugia*, 114, in *Omnibus*, 3rd ed., Marion Habig, ed. (Cincinnati: St. Anthony Messenger Press, 2008), pp. 1088–1089.

8. *Legend of Perugia*, 115, p. 1089.

9. Augustine, *Tractates on the Gospel of John* 65.2, in John W. Retting, trans., *The Fathers of the Church*, vol. 90 (Washington, D.C.: Catholic University of America Press, 1994), p. 51.

10. Thomas à Kempis, *Imitation of Christ*, 3, 5 (Dublin, Ireland: St. Paul's, 1993), p. 99.

11. Origen, *Commentary on the Epistle to the Romans* 5.8.13, in Thomas P. Scheck, trans., *The Fathers of the Church*, vol. 103 (Washington, D.C.: Catholic University of America Press, 2001), p. 359.

12. Dorotheos of Gaza, "On Renunciation," *Discourses and Sayings* 1, Eric P. Wheeler, trans. (Kalamazoo, Mich.: Cistercian, 1977), p. 88.

13. Søren Kierkegaard, *Søren Kierkegaard's Journals and Paper*, vol. 1, no. 538, Howard and Edna Wong, eds. and trans. (Bloomington: Indiana University Press, 1967), p. 219.

14. *Odes of and Psalms of Solomon* 42, 8–10, J. Rendel Harris, trans. (Cambridge: Cambridge University Press, 1909), p. 137.

15. See *Lumen Gentium*, 12.

16. World Synod of Bishops, Rome, October 1980.

17. *Conchita: A Mother's Spiritual Diary*, M.M. Philipon, ed., A.J. Owen, trans. (New York, Alba, 1978), p. 246.

18. Paul Claudel, *The Tidings Brought to Mary* (L'Annonce faite à Marie), act 3, Wallace Fowlie, trans. and intro. (Chicago: Henry Regnery, 1960), p. 100.

19. Augustine, Sermon 34, sect. 6, *The Works of Saint Augustine*, vol. 2, Edmund Hill, trans., John E. Rotelle, ed. (New York: New City, 1990), p. 168.

20. Augustine, Exposition 2 of Psalm 32 [33], 8, in *The Works of Saint Augustine*, vol. 15, John E. Rotelle, ed., Maria Boulding, trans. (Hyde Park, N.Y.: New City, 2000), pp. 400–401.

21. See Matthew 5:21–44 for the repetition of these phrases.

22. *The Little Flowers of St. Francis* 18, in *Omnibus*, p. 1341.

23. *Considerations on the Holy Stigmata* 1, in *Omnibus*, p. 1430.

24. St. Augustine, *Commentary on the Gospel of John* 45.2.

25. See Søren Kierkegaard, *The Gospel of Suffering and the Lilies of the Field*, D. Swenson and L.M. Swenson, trans. (Minneapolis: Augsburg, 1948), p. 21ff.

26. Giacomo Leopardi, "The Infinite" ["L'Infinito"], in *Giacomo Leopardi: Selected Poems*, Thomas G. Bergin and Anne Paducci, trans. (Smyrna, Del.: Griffon House, 2003), p. 21.

27. Augustine, *Confessions* 1.1, p. 43.

28. Leopardi, "The Infinite," p. 21.

29. Part of the formula to describe Christ at the Council of Chalcedon; see Josef Neuner and Jacques Dupuis, eds., *The Christian Faith*, 7th ed. (New York: Alba, 2000), p. 226.

30. Henry Barclay Swete, *The Apocalypse of St. John*, 3rd ed. (London: Macmillan, 1917), p. 249.

31. Ambrose, *On the Holy Spirit* 3.112, Roy J. Deferrari, trans., *The Fathers of the Church*, vol. 44 (Washington, D.C.: Catholic University of America Press, 2002), p. 193.

32. *Dei Verbum*, 21.

33. Francis of Assisi, "Second Version of the Letter to the Faithful," 2, in *Francis and Clare: The Complete Works*, Regis J. Armstrong and Ignatius C. Brady, trans. (New York: Paulist, 1982), p. 67.

34. See Max Zerwick, *A Grammatical Analysis of the Greek New Testament*, Mary Grosvenor, trans. and rev. (Rome: Editrice Pontificio Istituto Biblico, 1988), p. 38.

35. Shakespeare, *Hamlet* 2.2.569.

36. Philo of Alexandria, "*Quis rerum divinarum heres*" (Who Is the Heir of Divine Things?) 266, in *Philo*, vol. 4, rev. ed., F.H. Colson and G.H. Whitaker, eds. and trans. (Cambridge, Mass.: Harvard University Press, 1939), p. 419.

37. *Lumen Gentium*, 35.

38. See "Pope Paul Addresses the Charismatic Renewal," *New Covenant*, July 1975, p. 25. The quote is taken from Ambrose's hymn "*Splendor paternae gloriae.*"

39. The Ignatius Bible translates this as "Ascribe power to God."

40. Origen, *Commentary on the Epistle to the Romans, Books 1–5*, 5.8.13, p. 359.

41. *Presbyterorum Ordinis*, 2.

42. Paul VI, address, general audience, November 29, 1972.

43. See Raniero Cantalamessa, *Sober Intoxication of the Spirit* (Cincinnati: Servant, 2005), p. 41ff.

44. *Lexikon für Theologie und Kirche*, vol. 7, s.v. "obex" (Freiburg im Breisgau: Herder-Verlag, 1993–2001), pp. 1081–1082.

45. Quoted in Ralph Martin, p. 16.

46. Cyril of Jerusalem, *Catechesis* 17, 19, in Leo P. McCauley and Anthony A. Stephenson, trans. *The Fathers of the Church*, vol. 64 (Washington D.C.: Catholic University of America Press, 1970), pp. 107–108.

47. See Karl Rahner, "Religious Enthusiasm and the Experience of Grace," in David Morland, trans., *Theological Investigations*, vol. 16 (New York: Seabury, 1979), pp. 37–38.

48. Karl Rahner, *The Spirit in the Church*, John Griffiths, trans. (London: Burns and Oates, 1979), p. 11.

49. *Pneumatology* (from the Greek) is "theology of the Spirit."

50. "To the city of Rome and the whole world." This standard opening for ancient Roman proclamations is now used to signify that a papal document or blessing is addressed not just to Rome but to the whole world.

51. John Paul II, *Dominum et Vivificantem* 25 (emphasis in the original Latin though not in the English translation at www.vatican.va). See also *Ad Gentes*, 4.

52. Irenaeus, *The Treatise of Irenaeus of Lugdunum against the Heresies* 3.24.1, F.R. Montgomery Hitchcock, trans. (London: Society for Promoting Christian Knowledge, 1916), pp. 144.

53. Pope Paul VI, "Address to the International Conference on the Catholic Charismatic Renewal," May 19, 1975.

54. Cyprian, *The Unity of the Church* 6, in Roy J. Deferrari, ed. and trans., *The Fathers of the Church*, vol. 36 (Washington D.C.: Catholic University of America Press, 1958), p. 100.

55. Erasmus, *Hyperaspistes*, in Cornelis Augustijn, *Erasmus: His Life, Works, and Influence*, J.C. Grayson, trans. (Toronto: University of Toronto Press, 1991), p. 182.

56. Antonio Rosmini (1797–1855), priest and philosopher who called for innovative social and juridical reforms. When two of his books were placed on the Index in 1849, he submitted to the Church's ruling. (His writings were soon after proclaimed free of censure.)

57. Primo Mazzolari (1890–1959), priest and famous preacher to the working classes, had a concern for social justice.

58. Lorenzo Milani (1923–1967), an educator of disadvantaged children and an advocate for conscientious objectors at a time when such a stand was unpopular.

59. Primo Mazzolari, newspaper article in *L'eco di Bergamo*, Easter season, 1951 (Marsha Daigle-Williamson, trans.).

60. Lorenzo Milani, letter to Nicola Pistelli (editor of *Politica*, a Catholic magazine in Florence), August 8, 1959 (Marsha Daigle-Williamson, trans.).

INDEX

SCRIPTURE INDEX

19:22	16	3:3	111
21:11	97	3:5	111
24:18	5	4:10	67
26:39	65	4:14b	67
		4:15	66
Mark		4:26	67
1:15	2	4:29	67
1:22	93	6	67
8:34	65	6:25b	68
8:36	77	6:26–27	68
9:34	105	6:34	68
10:17–22	3	6:35	68
11:12ff	11	6:60	68
12:7	23	6:67	128
		6:68	68
Luke		7:37–39	16
1:76	95	7:39	25
4:18	108	8:28	20, 24
6:20	109	8:50	35
6:24	109	8:58	24
10:23–24	71	13:19	21
15:7	17	13:34a	48
18:18–25	3	15:1–2	51
		15:2	11
John		15:26–27	87, 98
1:1a	23	15:27	104
1:12	111	16:12	123
1:14	84	18:4–5	21
1:17	46	18:4–6	22
1:26	95	19:30	24
1:27	108		
1:29	21, 96	**Acts**	
2:3b	33	1:5	114

2:1–4a	114	8:1–13	42
2:3	94	8:2	44
2:9–11	104–105	8:3	45
2:11	106	8:7	46
2:13b	116	8:13b	50
2:14	117	8:18	73
2:15–18	118	8:21–23	85
2:15a	116	8:23	85
2:16	98	8:29	15
2:17–18	99, 107	10:9	123
2:22–24	98, 122	13:3	34
2:23	105	13:14a	40
2:36	98, 122	15:1–2	57
2:38	105		
2:39	99	**1 Corinthians**	
2:41–42	124	1:28	28
2:47b	124	1:30	26–27
5:32	87	2:4	92
9:4b	5	2:4–5	93
10:38	65	4:10a	36
11:27	99	7:7	59
13:1–3	99	7:39	57
13:52	85	10:4	25
15:32	99	11:32	27
21:9–10	99	12	14
		12—14	119
		12:3b	123
Romans		12:29	99
1:4	25	14	102
3:28	10	14:1	103
5:5	115	14:1a	14
5:5b	47	14:3	103
6:14b	46	14:5	103
8:1–2	42	14:23–35	103

1 Peter

1:2	119
2:2	5
3:15	72
3:18	24, 50
5:14	27

2 Peter

1:21	89

1 John

1:1–2	84
2:14b	42
3:14a	47
4:4	42, 82
4:8b	115
4:13	26
5:13	83

Revelation

2—3	8
2:1–7	9
2:5a	9
2:7a	9
2:11a	9
2:17a	9
2:20	13
2:22ff	13
2:29	9
3:2–3	10
3:6	9
3:13	9
3:14–22	9
3:19b	10
3:22	9
19:10	88
21:2	126–127

About the Author

Raniero Cantalamessa, O.F.M. CAP., was appointed by John Paul II as preacher to the papal household in 1980, and he continues to serve in that capacity for Pope Benedict XVI. He is the author of many books, including *Intoxication of the Spirit: Filled With the Fullness of God* and *The Beatitudes: Eight Steps to Happiness.*

About the Translator

Marsha Daigle-Williamson received her doctorate in comparative literature from the University of Michigan and is professor emerita of English at Spring Arbor University.